All You Need to Know about

The paleo diet is the best way you can eat as you are simply permitted to eat what our far off progenitors ate. The paleo diet, otherwise called Stone Age diet or the mountain man diet is essentially the main eating routine that makes your hereditary qualities work for yourself and assists you with remaining solid, dainty and healthy.

Now, that doesn't mean you need to develop the time machine and chase mammoths! It basically implies that practically every one of the food sources that were not accessible to our mountain men progenitors are off the table. A wide range of sorts of examination have demonstrated that it is our advanced items brimming with trans fats and sugar that are the reason for some infections including obesity.

So, how treats pass on you to eat while being on the paleo diet? All things considered, recollect the times of hunting and assembling. Your paleo menu ought to fundamentally comprise of natural products, vegetables, meats, fish, nuts. There is likewise a rundown of items that are not permitted on the paleo diet: grains, vegetables, handled food sources, potatoes, dairy, refined sugar, unhealthy food. For a portion of my plans I use grass-took care of spread and crude milk, these items actually can be utilized for this eating regimen. In any case, many individuals that are on a paleo diet actually consume dairy items. On the off chance that your body acknowledges milk, margarine, and yogurt - you are free to remember it for your ordinary meal.

I won't delve into subtleties here on how precisely the paleo diet functions and on what it changes in your body, I am not a specialist. Notwithstanding, let me list the primary advantages of this diet:

- Weight loss
- Less inflammation
- Better sleep
- Better mental health
-

- More energy
- Reduced exposure to toxins
- More vitamins and minerals
- Eco-friendly living

While the paleo diet might appear to be restricting when you contemplate every one of the various food sources you will not have the option to appreciate, it is undeniably less restricting than some other calorie-counting diet plan. It is likewise one of the advantages of this cave dweller diet - you don't need to count calories. The paleo diet considers that we are largely unique and that each individual has individual requirements with regards to calories. Consequently, you don't need to stress over calories any longer as long as you eat entire, normal food sources. For the people who are intrigued, however, this book has complete dietary data for every formula, which will be useful assuming you're focusing on certain macronutrient ratios.

Still, the paleo diet is certifiably not an enchanted one, and it is likewise vital to do a few actual activities to get thinner and to remain fit. It is firmly prescribed to coordinate development into your daily existence. There is no unique wellness plan for this eating regimen, simply recollect that our progenitors had an extremely dynamic life. Attempt to walk more, climb, bicycle, swim or some other action you prefer.

I like the Paleo diet since it is a lot more straightforward than some other eating routine I have been on. So don't fear changing your dietary patterns, and you will see the results!

Paleo Diet Tips

1. **Movement is more important than exercises**

Paleo diet doesn't expect you to go through hours in the rec center and practicing a great deal. It is more critical to incorporate development into your regular daily existence. Attempt to walk more, take a stab at climbing, trekking, swimming or some other action you prefer.

Take steps as opposed to taking a lift, leave your vehicle a piece father and stroll to your office. You will before long see it isn't so much that that difficult.

2. Do not hurry up

Make the progress to paleo diet as smooth as could be expected. You don't need to discard all non-paleo food at a time. Start by making paleo breakfast first, then lunch, and then dinner. You can likewise transform one-two dinners a week.

3. Make a plan for the first two weeks

Find the best plans for you and make a suppers arrangement for the initial fourteen days of your paleo eating less junk food. Make a shopping list for itself and get all that you will require. Accordingly, it will be simpler for you to begin. Additionally, there will be less compulsion to cook something non-paleo, as you will have every one of the items purchased already.

4. Get enough sleep

If you don't get sufficient rest or the nature of your rest is poor, it will be more hard for you to begin shedding pounds. Consequently, ensure you do rest competently and enough. Plus, it is essential to diminish pressure, particularly in the start of your paleo way.

5. You need to stay hydrated all the time

Specialists suggest drinking 16 oz of water in the main hour once you awaken and add another 16-20 oz of water before early afternoon. To remain appropriately hydrated you ought to drink something like 60-70 ounces of water on an every day basis.

6. Prepare paleo snacks

Anticipate getting eager and consistently have a few tidbits arranged. To swindle make a timetable for paleo snacks and pick when you feel hungry between fundamental meals.

7. No limits, try substitution instead

You don't need to limit from treats or a few other most loved suppers. Simply find a substitute for non-paleo fixings. Use coconut milk rather than a customary one, coconut flour rather than generally useful flour. Sugar can be subbed with crude honey or maple syrup. Every one of the plans in this book are 100 percent paleo and you will utilize just paleo amicable items to cook your most loved dishes

8. Practice intermittent fasting

Intermittent fasting would be exceptionally useful for fat misfortune. It is impossible that our predecessors had three suppers every day. So you can likewise attempt to quick a bit.

Instant Pot Useful Tips

1. Start with carefully reading the instructions for your device

Every strain cooker accompanies a manual that you ought to painstakingly study, as it contains terms of utilization, extra helpful hints, and, in particular, data on how use it safely.

2. Store it right

After completing your cooking, wash the cooker and put away it. Try to really take a look at the valves and clean those as well.

3. Do not forget to add liquid

Pressure cooker needs fluid to develop steam tension inside to really prepare the food. This implies you want to try to add fluid to the ingredients.

4. Do not overfill the cooker

All advanced tension cookers have least and greatest imprints within the cooking pot. Try not to surpass those. While cooking with fluid try to abstain from filling the greater part full, as filling more that can prompt spill.

5. Right heat

You should make a point to pick the right hotness for cooking, as it is one of the vital components for effective cooking in the strain cooker. Check the required formula for more details.

6. Right timing

You should make a point to pick the right planning for cooking, as it is one of the vital components for fruitful cooking in the strain cooker. Check the required formula for more details.

7. Brown the ingredients

Ingredients in the strain cooker don't brown, so make a point to really brown those before you begin cooking. Assuming you have an advanced electric tension cooker you can do that in it as well.

8. Slice the ingredients to the right size

Slice food into even pieces for cooking. Bigger cuts will cook more slow, more modest cuts quicker. Check the required formula for more details.

9. Release the pressure

There are typically two methods for delivering steam in your tension cooker: a) turning a strain discharge valve - use broiler gloves for this as hot steam will rush out, and c) or open the top cover. Nonetheless, make a point to painstakingly open the top cover not to get burnt.

Metric Conversion

Mexican Chicken Breasts

Cooking time: 11 minutes

Servings: 4

Ingredients:

- 4 chicken breasts, skinless, cut into strips
- 2 tablespoons olive oil
- ½ cup cilantro
- 1 lime, juiced
- 1 teaspoon raw honey
- ¼ teaspoon cumin
- 1 yellow onion, chopped
- 3 garlic cloves, minced
- 3 tomatoes, peeled and chopped
- 2 tablespoons parsley, chopped
- 1 teaspoon garlic powder
- 1 tablespoon onion powder
- 1 tablespoon chili powder
- ½ cup water or chicken stock

- A pinch of sea salt and black pepper

Instructions:

1. Add oil to your Instant pot and press "Sauté" button, heat it up.
2. Add onion and garlic, mix and sauté for 3 minutes with the top open.
3. Press "Keep warm/Cancel" button. Add chicken, cilantro, lime juice, honey, cumin, tomatoes, salt, pepper, parsley, garlic powder, water or stock, onion and stew powder, mix well.
4. Close the cover, and turn the vent to "Sealed".
5. Press "Manual" button, set the clock for 8 minutes and set "Strain" to high.
6. Once the clock is up, press "Drop" button and permit the strain to be delivered normally, until the float valve drops down.
7. Open the lid.
   NOTE: Make sure the tension is completely delivered prior to opening the top, so you don't get burnt.

Nutritional info:

Calories: 243

Fats (g): 20.4

Fiber (g): 2.7

Net carbs (g): 7

Protein (g): 15.7

Cherry Tomato Chicken Cacciatore

Cooking time: 25 minutes

Servings: 4

Ingredients:

- 3 pounds chicken legs with thighs
- 2 garlic cloves, crushed
- 1 teaspoon salt
- 1 teaspoon olive oil

- ¼ teaspoon hot pepper flakes
- 1 pound cherry tomatoes, stems removed
- 1 cup water
- 2 tablespoons dry red wine
- 1 teaspoon dried oregano
- ½ cup green olives, cut in half
- 1 sprig fresh basil leaves, torn

Instructions:

1. Press "Sauté" button on the tension cooker and hotness it up. Add olive oil and chicken thighs, cook for 6-7 minutes the two sides with the cover open until all sides are browned.
2. Put cherry tomatoes into a Ziploc sack. Zip the pack and delicately squash the tomatoes utilizing something heavy.
3. Transfer seared chicken thighs to a plate.
4. Put the squashed tomatoes and juices to the strain cooker.
5. Add oregano, garlic, water, wine, salt and hot pepper. Blend well.
6. Put chicken back to the cooker. Blend and coat chicken with the sauce.
7. Press "Keep warm/Cancel" button. Close the top, and turn the vent to "Sealed".
8. Press "Manual" button, set the clock for 14 minutes and set "Tension" to high.
9. Once the clock is up press "Drop" button and hang tight for 10 minutes for the strain to go down a bit.
10. Turn the steam discharge handle to "Venting" position for speedy delivery, until the float valve drops down.
11. Open the lid.
    NOTE: Make sure the tension is completely delivered prior to opening the top, so you don't get burnt.
12. Sprinkle with basil and green olives on top before serving.

Nutritional info:

Calories: 443

Fats (g): 53

Fiber (g): 1.6 Net
carbs (g): 5.6
Protein (g): 25.7

Sweet Chicken Wings

Cooking time: 20 minutes
Servings: 4

Ingredients:

- 2 pounds chicken wings
- 1 lime, juiced
- 3 tablespoons raw honey
- 2 tablespoons coconut aminos
- ½ cup water
- salt, to taste

Instructions:

1. Mix lime juice, honey, aminos and salt in a medium bowl.
2. Put chicken wings to into a Ziploc pack, add marinade. Marinate for an hour in a fridge.
3. Put chicken and marinade to the Instant Pot, add water. Close the top, and turn the vent to "Sealed".
4. Press "Manual" button, set the clock for 15 minutes and set "Strain" to high.
5. Once the clock is up press "Drop" button and turn the steam discharge handle to "Venting" position for speedy delivery, until the float valve drops down.
6. Open the lid.
   NOTE: Make sure the tension is completely delivered prior to opening the cover, so you don't get burnt.
7. Remove the fluid from the tension cooker, leave about ½ cups inside.

8. Press "Sauté" button and let the wings to cook for 5 additional minutes.
   Press "Keep warm/Cancel" button.
9. Add eliminated fluid, mix well and serve.

Nutritional info:

Calories: 485

Fats (g): 46.8

Fiber (g): 0.1

Net carbs (g): 14.7

Protein (g): 35.7

Japanese Chicken Thighs

Cooking time: 25 minutes

Servings: 6

Ingredients:

- 2 pounds chicken thighs, skinless
-

- 2 tablespoons olive oil
- 2 teaspoons arrowroot starch, dissolved in ¼ cup of water
- 1 cup vegetable or chicken broth
- 1 onion, chopped
- 1 garlic clove, minced
- 1 tablespoon minced ginger

For sauce:

- ½ tablespoon minced garlic
- 1 tablespoon unseasoned rice vinegar
- 1 tablespoon fresh ginger, minced
- ½ cup gochujang
- ¼ cup hoisin sauce
- ¼ cup mirin
- ¼ cup soy sauce
- 1 tablespoon organic ketchup
- ¼ cup rice wine

Instructions:

1. Press "Sauté" button on the strain cooker, add oil and hotness it up.
2. Add chicken thighs, cook for 6-7 minutes the two sides with the top open until all sides are carmelized. Eliminate chicken from the cooker.
3. Put garlic, ginger and onion to the Instant Pot. Sauté for 3 minutes. Set the chicken pieces back to the skillet and pess "Keep warm/Cancel" button.
4. Mix all sauce fixings in a bowl.
5. Reserve a cup of the sauce and put the rest to the Instant pot, add stock. Close the top, and turn the vent to "Sealed".
6. Press "Manual" button, set the clock for 17 minutes and set "Strain" to high.
7. Once the clock is up press "Drop" button and turn the steam discharge handle to "Venting" position for speedy delivery, until the

float valve drops down.
8. Open the lid.
NOTE: Make sure the tension is completely delivered prior to opening the top, so you don't get burnt.
9. Stir in the remainder of the sauce and broke up arrowroot starch combination, blend well until the sauce thickens.
10. Serve chicken with the sauce.

Nutritional info:

Calories: 246

Fats (g): 37

Fiber (g): 1

Net carbs (g): 17

Protein (g): 33

Spicy Garlic Chicken

Cooking time: 25 minutes

Servings: 4

Ingredients:

- 3 pounds chicken thighs, skinless
- 1 teaspoon chili garlic sauce
- ¾ cup organic ketchup
- ¾ cup soy sauce
- ½ cup water or chicken stock
- 1 tablespoon fresh basil, chopped
- 2 tablespoons arrowroot starch, dissolved in 2 tablespoons of water
- ½ teaspoon garlic cloves, minced

Instructions:

1. Press "Sauté" button on the strain cooker, add oil and hotness it up.
2. Add chicken thighs, cook for 6-7 minutes the two sides with the

cover open until all sides are seared. Press "Keep warm/Cancel" button.
3. Add soy sauce, stew sauce, garlic, water or stock and natural ketchup to the pot. Mix the fixings and close the top, turn the vent to "Sealed".
4. Press "Manual" button, set the clock for 10 minutes and set "Tension" to high.
5. Once the clock is up press "Drop" button and turn the steam discharge handle to "Venting" position for speedy delivery, until the float valve drops down.
6. Open the lid.
NOTE: Make sure the strain is completely delivered prior to opening the cover, so you don't get burnt.
7. Transfer the meat to a plate. Add arrowroot starch blend to the pot. Press "Sauté" button on the tension cooker and mix until the sauce thickens.
8. Pour the sauce over the meat before serving.

Nutritional info:

Calories: 532

Fats (g): 55.4

Fiber (g): 0.7

Net carbs (g): 15.2

Protein (g): 30.2

Garlic Ginger Chicken with Bok Choy

Cooking time: 20 minutes

Servings: 3

Ingredients:

- 1 pound chicken breast, cooked and shredded
- 4 pounds Bok Choy, chopped
- 2 tablespoons coconut oil
- 2 tablespoons ginger, minced

- 1 ½ cups homemade unsalted chicken stock
- salt, pepper, to taste
- 2 tablespoons garlic, minced

Instructions:

1. Press "Sauté" button on the strain cooker, add oil and hotness it up.
2. Add garlic and ginger, sauté until carmelized a piece, with the top open.
3. Add Bok Choy and sauté for 5 additional minutes. Press "Keep warm/Cancel" button.
4. Add chicken and stock, salt and pepper, mix well. Close the cover, and turn the vent to "Sealed".
5. Press "Manual" button, set the clock for 10 minutes and set "Strain" to high.
6. Once the clock is up press "Drop" button and turn the steam discharge handle to "Venting" position for speedy delivery, until the float valve drops down.
7. Open the lid.
   NOTE: Make sure the tension is completely delivered prior to opening the top, so you don't get burnt.

Nutritional info:

Calories: 393

Fats (g): 25.4

Fiber (g): 3.6

Net carbs (g): 11.8

Protein (g): 14.8

Tarragon Chicken Breasts

Cooking time: 15 minutes

Servings: 4

Ingredients:

- 4 chicken breasts, halved
- ½ cup white wine
- ½ cup water or chicken stock
- 1 teaspoon fresh tarragon
- 1 tablespoon olive oil
- 1 tablespoon Worcestershire sauce
- ¼ cup onion, chopped
- 1 tablespoon arrowroot starch, dissolved in ¼ cup of cold water
- ¼ cup celery, sliced

- ¼ cup carrot, sliced
- 1 teaspoon salt
- ¼ teaspoon black pepper

Instructions:

1. Press "Sauté" button on the strain cooker, add oil and hotness it up.
2. Add chicken bosoms, cook for 6-7 minutes the two sides with the top open until all sides are carmelized. Press "Keep warm/Cancel" button.
3. Add wine, tarragon, Worcestershire sauce, onion, celery, carrot, salt, pepper and water or stock. Close the top, and turn the vent to "Sealed".
4. Press "Manual" button, set the clock for 7 minutes and set "Strain" to high.
5. Once the clock is up, press "Drop" button and permit the strain to be delivered normally, until the float valve drops down.
6. Open the lid.
   NOTE: Make sure the tension is completely delivered prior to opening the top, so you don't get burnt. Put the cooked meat to a platter and cover with foil.
7. Press "Sauté" button on the tension cooker. Add arrowroot starch combination to the pot, mix well with the top open until the sauce thickens.
8. Serve the meat with the sauce.

Nutritional info:

Calories: 207

Fats (g): 26.3

Fiber (g): 0.6 Net

carbs (g): 6.8

Protein (g): 14

California Chicken

Cooking time: 15 minutes

Servings: 6

Ingredients:

- 6 chicken breast halves, boneless and skinless
- 1 teaspoon rosemary
- 3 garlic cloves, peeled and sliced
- ¼ cup parsley, chopped
- ½ cup chicken broth
- ½ cup white wine
- 2 tablespoons olive oil
- salt and pepper, to taste
- ½ lemon, thinly sliced

Instructions:

1. Press "Sauté" button on the tension cooker, add oil and hotness it up.
2. Add chicken bosoms, cook for 6-7 minutes the two sides with the top open until all sides are browned.
3. Season the chicken with rosemary and add garlic. Press "Keep warm/Cancel" button.
4. Mix wine, stock and parsley in a bowl. Add the combination to the pot.
5. Close the top, and turn the vent to "Sealed".
6. Press "Manual" button, set the clock for 8 minutes and set "Strain" to high.
7. Once the clock is up press "Drop" button and turn the steam discharge handle to "Venting" position for speedy delivery, until the float valve drops down.
8. Open the lid.
   NOTE: Make sure the tension is completely delivered prior to opening the cover, so you don't get burnt.
9. Put lemon cuts on top before serving.

Nutritional info:

Calories: 192

Fats (g): 27.7

Fiber (g): 0.4 Net

carbs (g): 1.9

Protein (g): 14.4

Sweet and Sour Chicken

Cooking time: 25 minutes

Servings: 5

Ingredients:

- 3 pounds chicken (any part), skinless, cut into bite-size pieces
- ¼ teaspoon ground ginger
- 1 can pineapple chunks, with juice
- 2 tablespoons soy sauce
- 1 tablespoon raw honey
- 1 green pepper, chunked
- ½ cup vinegar
- ½ cup celery, sliced
- ½ teaspoon Worcestershire sauce
- 1 tablespoon olive oil

Instructions:

1. Press "Sauté" button on the tension cooker, add oil and hotness it up.
2. Add chicken bosoms, cook for 6-7 minutes the two sides with the top open until all sides are seared. Press "Keep warm/Cancel" button.
3. Add ginger, pineapple, soy sauce, honey, green pepper, vinegar, celery and Worcestershire sauce. Close the top, and turn the vent to "Sealed".
4. Press "Manual" button, set the clock for 12 minutes and set "Strain" to high.

5. Once the clock is up press "Drop" button and turn the steam discharge handle to "Venting" position for fast delivery, until the float valve drops down.
6. Open the lid.
   NOTE: Make sure the tension is completely delivered prior to opening the cover, so you don't get burnt.

Nutritional info:

Calories: 480

Fats (g): 31.2

Fiber (g): 1.1

Net carbs (g): 10.1

Protein (g): 19.7

Chinese Style Shredded Chicken

Cooking time: 30 minutes

Servings: 4

Ingredients:

- 8 to 10 pieces chicken drumsticks
- 2 stalks green onion, chopped
- 10 pieces dried Chinese red chili
- 1 tablespoon ginger, chopped
- 3 cloves garlic,
- minced 1 tablespoon
- olive oil 2 tablespoons
  honey
- ¼ cup dark soy sauce
- 1 teaspoon sesame oil
- 2 tablespoons arrowroot starch, dissolved in 2 tablespoons of water
- 2 tablespoons Chinese black vinegar
- 2 tablespoons Shaoxing wine

Instructions:

1. Press "Sauté" button on the tension cooker, add oil and hotness it up. Add chicken and cook until brown, for 2-3 minutes on each side. Move meat to a plate.
2. Add garlic and white piece of green onion to the Instant pot, sauté for 2 minutes with the top open.
3. Add hacked ginger and red stew and cook for an additional 3 minutes. Press "Keep warm/Cancel" button.
4. Add honey, soy sauce, sesame oil, dark vinegar and Shaoxing wine to a bowl. Blend well until combined.
5. Add the combination to the pot, add chicken. Close the top, and turn the vent to "Sealed".
6. Press "Manual" button, set the clock for 15 minutes and set "Strain" to high.
7. Once the clock is up, press "Drop" button and permit the strain to be delivered normally, until the float valve drops down.
8. Open the lid.

NOTE: Make sure the tension is completely delivered prior to opening the top, so you don't get burnt.

9. Transfer the cooked meat to a bowl. Shred it utilizing a fork and dispose of the bones.
10. Remove red stew from the pot. Press "Sauté" button on the cooker and carry the blend to a boil.
11. Slowly add the arrowroot starch combination while continually mixing. Set the meat back to the pot once the sauce thickens. Blend well and add red chili.
12. Turn the Instant Pot off after 1-2 minutes.

Nutritional info:

Calories: 333

Fats (g): 28.6

Fiber (g): 1

Net carbs (g): 10.9

Protein (g): 14.7

Thai Chicken Soup

Cooking time: 10 minutes

Servings: 6

Ingredients:

- 1 pound chicken breast, cut into 1-inch slices
- 1 tablespoon coconut oil
- 1 onion, chopped
- 1 jalapeno, chopped
- 1 tablespoon curry paste
- 1 can full fat coconut milk
- 2 zucchinis, spiralized
- 2 tablespoon fish sauce
- 1 lime, juiced

- 8 cups chicken broth
- salt, to taste

Instructions:

1. Add oil to the Instant pot and press "Sauté" button. Add onion, cook for 2-3 minutes until soft.
2. Add jalapeno and garlic, cook for 1-2 additional minutes. Add chicken, curry glue and coconut milk, sauté for another 2-3 minutes.
3. Press "Keep warm/Cancel" button, add fish sauce, stock and salt.
4. Close the cover, and turn the vent to "Sealed".
5. Press "Manual" button, set the clock for 5 minutes and set "Strain" to high.
6. Once the clock is up press "Drop" button and turn the steam discharge handle to "Venting" position for speedy delivery, until the float valve drops down.
7. *Open the lid.*
   NOTE: Make sure the tension is completely delivered prior to opening the top, so you don't get burnt.
8. Add zoodles to the Instant pot and blend well, continue to blend for 1-2 minutes. Serve soup with lime juice.

Nutritional info:

Calories: 218

Fats (g): 12.6

Fiber (g): 1.5 Net

carbs (g): 7.7

Protein (g): 24.2

Chicken Tomatillo Stew

Cooking time: 20 minutes

Servings: 6

Ingredients:

- 2 pounds chicken breast, cooked and shredded
- 1 can tomatillos, drained and chopped
- 1 tablespoon coconut oil
- 2 garlic cloves, minced
- 2 poblano peppers, chopped
- 2 bell peppers, chopped
- 1 yellow onion, chopped
- 2 teaspoons chili powder
- 1 teaspoon paprika
- 1 teaspoon chipotle powder
- 4 cups chicken broth
- 1 teaspoon cumin
- 2 Jalapeno pepper, chopped

Instructions:

1. Press "Sauté" button on the tension cooker, add oil and hotness it up.
2. Add onion and garlic, poblano peppers, Jalapeno pepper and chime peppers, sauté until onions are clear, with the top open.
3. Add every one of the flavors: bean stew powder, paprika, chipotle powder and cumin. Blend well.
4. Add tomatillos, chicken and chicken stock. Bring to a stew, press "Keep warm/Cancel" button and close the cover, turn the vent to "Sealed".
5. Press "Manual" button, set the clock for 15 minutes and set "Tension" to high.
6. Once the clock is up, press "Drop" button and permit the strain to be delivered normally, until the float valve drops down.
7. Open the lid.
   NOTE: Make sure the strain is completely delivered prior to opening the top, so you don't get burnt.
8. Adjust flavors if necessary and serve.

Nutritional info:
Calories: 255
Fats (g): 27.5
Fiber (g): 2
Net carbs (g): 8.8
Protein (g): 16.6

Curried Chicken Salad

Cooking time: 5 minutes
Servings: 3

Ingredients:

- 1 rib celery, sliced
- 1 onion, peeled and
- quartered 6-8 peppercorns

- 1 cup water
- 3 tablespoons curry powder
- 2 chicken breasts, halved
- ¾ cup organic mayonnaise
- 1 cup apples, diced
- ½ cup toasted slivered almonds
- salt and pepper to taste
- 1 carrot, peeled and sliced

Instructions:

1. Pour water into the strain cooker. Add peppercorns, carrot, onion and celery.
2. Place a trivet inside the cooker. Set the meat on top.
3. Close the cover and press "Manual" button, set the clock for 5 minutes and set "Tension" to high.
4. Once the clock is up, press "Drop" button and permit the strain to be delivered normally, until the float valve drops down.
5. Open the lid.
   NOTE: Make sure the strain is completely delivered prior to opening the top, so you don't get burnt.
6. Put the meat into a bowl. Strain the fluid from the Instant Pot and pour this over the meat. Permit to cool.
7. Remove the meat from the fluid. Dispose of the skin and eliminate bones. Shred the meat.
8. Mix curry powder, mayonnaise, pepper and salt in a bowl. Add toasted almonds, onions, celery and apples. Add chicken meat and blend well.
9. Allow to cool in the refrigerator before serving.

Nutritional info:

Calories: 473

Fats (g): 33.5

Fiber (g): 3.6 Net

carbs (g): 5.2

Protein (g): 21.1

Mediterranean Chicken Thighs

Cooking time: 25 minutes

Servings: 4

Ingredients:

- 3 pounds chicken thighs, skinless 1
- can black olives, sliced
- 1 tablespoon parsley, chopped 1
- tablespoon garlic, chopped 1
- tablespoon olive oil
- 1 cup chicken broth 1
- cup onion, chopped 1
- teaspoon basil
- 1 teaspoon oregano
- ½ cup celery leaves, chopped
- 2 tablespoons arrowroot starch, dissolved in 2 tablespoons of cold water
- salt and pepper to taste

Instructions:

1. Press "Sauté" button on the tension cooker, add oil and hotness it up.
2. Add onion and garlic, cook for 2-3 minutes with the top open. Move to a bowl.
3. Put chicken thighs to the pot and cook for 6-7 minutes the two sides with the top open until sautéed. Press "Keep warm/Cancel" button, set cooked onion and garlic back to the pot.
4. Add stock and add oregano, celery, basil and parsley. Blend well and close the lid.
5. Press "Manual" button, set the clock for 12 minutes and

set "Strain" to high.
6. Once the clock is up press "Drop" button and turn the steam discharge handle to "Venting" position for fast delivery, until the float valve drops down.
7. Open the lid.
   NOTE: Make sure the tension is completely delivered prior to opening the cover, so you don't get burnt.
8. Remove the chicken thighs from the cooker and press "Sauté" button.
9. Add olives to the Instant pot and mix in the arrowroot starch combination. Stew until the sauce thickens.
10. Serve the meat with sauce.

Nutritional info:

Calories: 398

Fats (g): 37

Fiber (g): 1.1 Net

carbs (g): 5.8

Protein (g): 17.1

Chicken Vegetable Soup

Cooking time: 25 minutes

Servings: 6

Ingredients:

- 1 pound chicken meat, cooked, shredded
- 2 tablespoons olive oil
- 1 onion, chopped
- 1 carrot, diced
- 7 oz mushrooms, sliced
- 6 cups chicken stock
- 3 garlic cloves, chopped
- 1 teaspoon thyme
- 1 teaspoon rosemary

- 2 bay leaves
- salt and pepper to taste

Instructions:

1. Add oil to Instant Pot and press "Sauté" button. Add onion and cook for 1-2 minutes until soft.
2. Add carrots and garlic, cook for 2-3 additional minutes. Add mushrooms and cook for 3 additional minutes.
3. Press "Keep warm/Cancel" button and add chicken to the Instant pot, likewise stock, thyme, rosemary, inlet leaves, salt and pepper.
4. Close the cover, and turn the vent to "Fixed". Press "Soup" button and change clock to 20 minutes.
5. Once the clock is up press "Drop" button and turn the steam discharge handle to "Venting" position for fast delivery, until the float valve drops down.
6. Open the lid.
   NOTE: Make sure the strain is completely delivered prior to opening the cover, so you don't get burnt.

Nutritional info:

Calories: 216

Fats (g): 11

Fiber (g): 1.2 Net

carbs (g): 5.4

Protein (g): 24

Chicken Pina Colada

Cooking time: 15 minutes
Servings: 4

Ingredients:

- 2 pounds chicken thighs, cut into chunks
- ½ cup full fat coconut cream
- ½ cup chicken stock
- 2 tablespoons coconut aminos
- 1/8 teaspoon salt
- 1 cup pineapple chunks, fresh or frozen
- 1 teaspoon cinnamon
- ½ cup green onion, chopped

Instructions:

1. Put chicken thighs, pineapple pieces, cinnamon and salt into the

Instant Pot.
2. Add coconut cream, coconut aminos and stock.
3. Close the top. Press "Poultry" button, cook for 15 minutes (the Instant Pot will set the tension automatically).
4. Once the clock is up, press "Drop" button and permit the strain to be delivered normally, until the float valve drops down.
5. Open the lid.
   NOTE: Make sure the strain is completely delivered prior to opening the cover, so you don't get burnt.
6. Serve meat with the fluid sauce and embellishment with green onion.

Nutritional info:

Calories: 665

Fats (g): 36.9

Fiber (g): 1.2

Net carbs (g): 12.8

Protein (g): 18

Chicken Barbeque Wings

Cooking time: 45 minutes

Servings: 5

Ingredients:

- 4 pounds chicken wings, excess skin removed
- 1 tablespoon paprika
- 4 teaspoons chili powder
- 1 teaspoon garlic powder
- 1 teaspoon onion powder
- 1 teaspoon cumin
- 1 teaspoon rosemary
- 2 cups organic ketchup
- 3 garlic gloves, minced

- 3 tablespoons coconut oil
- ¼ cup white wine vinegar
- 1 small onion, minced
- 1/3 cup Worcestershire sauce
- 1 teaspoon cayenne pepper
- ¼ cup honey
- salt, pepper, to taste

Instructions:

1. Mix paprika, 2 teaspoons bean stew powder, garlic powder, onion powder, cumin and rosemary in a bowl.
2. Rub the chicken wings with the zest blend and set aside.
3. Press "Sauté" button on the tension cooker, add oil and hotness it up.
4. Add garlic and onion, sauté for quite some time with the top open until they are soft.
5. Add natural ketchup, white wine vinegar, Worcestershire sauce, cayenne pepper, honey, salt and pepper and blend well.
6. Cook the sauce for 30 minutes with the top open, let it stew. Press "Keep warm/Cancel" button.
7. Add chicken wings, press "Poultry" button and set the clock for 10 minutes.
8. Once the clock is up, press "Drop" button and permit the strain to be delivered normally, until the float valve drops down.
9. Open the lid.
   NOTE: Make sure the tension is completely delivered prior to opening the cover, so you don't get burnt.
10. If you like fresh wings sear them in the broiler for a couple of moments on each side.

Nutritional info:

Calories: 557

Fats (g): 51

Fiber (g): 1.9 Net

carbs (g): 18

Protein (g): 56

Cranberry Turkey

Cooking time: 40 minutes

Servings: 4

Ingredients:

- 4 pounds turkey thighs or wings
- 1 ½ cups cranberries, fresh or frozen
- 1 tablespoon olive oil
- 1 teaspoon sea salt
- 1 teaspoon dried thyme
- 1 teaspoon ground cinnamon
- 1 small lemon, chopped, seeds removed
- 2 tablespoons arrowroot starch, dissolved in 2 tablespoons of water
- ¼ cup raisins
- 2 teaspoons water
- 3 garlic cloves, minced
- 1 cup apple cider
- ½ tablespoon dried parsley flakes

Instructions:

1. Press "Sauté" button on the strain cooker, add oil, garlic and raisins to the pot, sauté for 2-3 minutes with the top open.
2. Add the meat into the skillet; put lemon and 1 cup of cranberries on top of the turkey. Press "Keep warm/Cancel" buttonю
3. Mix apple juice, ground cinnamon, thyme, parsley pieces and ocean salt in a bowl. Add the blend to the pot. Close the cover, and turn the vent to "Sealed"..
4. Press "Poultry" button and set the clock for 30 minutes.
5. Once the clock is up, press "Drop" button and permit the strain to be

delivered normally, until the float valve drops down.
6. Open the lid.
   NOTE: Make sure the tension is completely delivered prior to opening the top, so you don't get burnt.
7. Preheat the stove grill. Move the cooked turkey to a goulash. Sear in the broiler for 5 minutes.
8. Press "Sauté" button on the strain cooker. Add the excess cranberries to the sauce.
9. Add the combination of arrowroot flour and water. Mix the sauce and permit to stew until it thickens a bit.
10. Serve the carmelized turkey pieces with the cranberry sauce.

Nutritional info:
Calories: 287
Fats (g): 23.7
Fiber (g): 2
Net carbs (g): 19
Protein (g): 21.7

Turkey Breasts with Veggies and Gravy

Cooking time: 50 minutes
Servings: 4

Ingredients:

- 5 pound turkey breast, skinless
- 1 carrot, diced
- 1 onion, diced
- 1 celery rib, diced
- 1 garlic clove, smashed and
- peeled 2 teaspoons dried sage
- 2 tablespoons ghee
- 1 bay leaf
- ¼ cup dry white wine
- 1 ½ cups organic bone broth
- salt and pepper, to taste

Instructions:

1. Pat the meat with paper towels to dry. Liberally rub all leaves behind salt and pepper.
2. Press "Sauté" button on the strain cooker and liquefy the ghee. Brown each side of the meat for 5 minutes with the top open. Move turkey to a plate, leave fat in the pot.
3. Sauté celery, carrot and onion in the pot for 5 minutes. Add sage and garlic, cook for another minute.
4. Add wine and cook for 3 minutes. Add inlet leaf and stock. Mix the dish and scratch the lower part of the container. Put the turkey with the skin side up. Press "Keep warm/Cancel" button.
5. Close the cover, and turn the vent to "Fixed". Press "Manual" button, set the clock for 35 minutes and set "Strain" to high.
6. Once the clock is up press "Drop" button and turn the steam discharge handle to "Venting" position for speedy delivery, until the float valve drops down.
7. Open the lid.
   NOTE: Make sure the tension is completely delivered prior to opening the cover, so you don't get burnt.
8. Transfer the meat to a plate. Freely cover with foil. Utilize a drenching blender to make a puree from the cooking fluid and veggies in the pot.
9. Press "Sauté" button on the strain cooker and cook the puree for 3-5 minutes mixing continually. Season to taste.
10. Slice the meat and pour the sauce on top before serving.

Nutritional info:

Calories: 454
Fats (g): 42.7
Fiber (g): 3.3
Net carbs (g): 13.4
Protein (g): 30.6

Turkey Leftover Soup

Cooking time: 12 minutes

Servings: 6-8

Ingredients:

- 1 pound turkey meat, cooked, shredded
- ½ cauliflower head, chopped
- 2 carrots, diced
- 2 celery stalks, diced
- 1 onion, diced
- 3 garlic cloves, halved
- 1 tablespoon parsley, chopped
- 1 cup spinach
- 8 cups chicken or turkey broth
- 1 teaspoon oregano
- 1 teaspoon thyme
- salt and pepper, to taste

Instructions:

1. Add turkey meat, cauliflower, carrots, onion, celery, garlic, stock, oregano, thyme, salt and pepper to the Instant pot.
2. Close the top, and turn the vent to "Sealed".
3. Press "Manual" button, set the clock for 10 minutes and set "Strain" to high.
4. Once the clock is up, press "Drop" button and permit the strain to be delivered normally, until the float valve drops down.
5. Open the lid.
   NOTE: Make sure the tension is completely delivered prior to opening the cover, so you don't get burnt.
6. Add spinach to the Instant pot, mix for 1-2 minutes, add more salt and pepper if necessary and serve.

Nutritional info:

Calories: 437

Fats (g): 19.6

Fiber (g): 1.9
Net carbs (g): 6
Protein (g): 47.4

Plain Turkey Meatballs

Cooking time: 14 minutes
Servings: 4

Ingredients:

- 1 egg
- 1 pound ground turkey
- salt and black pepper, to taste
- ¼ cup almond flour
- ½ teaspoon garlic powder
- 1 cup water
- 2 tablespoons sun dried tomatoes, chopped
- 2 tablespoons olive oil
- 2 tablespoon basil, chopped

Instructions:

1. Mix turkey with salt, pepper, egg, flour, garlic powder, sun dried tomatoes and basil in a bowl.
2. Form the blend into twelve (2" each) meatballs.
3. Press "Sauté" button on the tension cooker, add oil and hotness it up.
4. Add meatballs and earthy colored them for 2 minutes on each side with the top open, press "Keep warm/Cancel" button then, at that point, move to a plate.
5. Add water to the tension cooker. Place a trivet or a liner bin inside. Put meatballs on a trivet or a bin and close the cover, turn the vent to "Sealed".
6. Press "Manual" button, set the clock for 5-6 minutes and set "Tension" to high.

7. Once the clock is up, press "Drop" button and permit the strain to be delivered normally, until the float valve drops down.
8. Open the lid.
NOTE: Make sure the tension is completely delivered prior to opening the top, so you don't get burnt.

Nutritional info:

Calories: 316

Fats (g): 33.1

Fiber (g): 0.5 Net

carbs (g): 1.6

Protein (g): 21.9

Herb Roasted Turkey Legs

Cooking time: 30 minutes

Servings: 4

Ingredients:

- 4 turkey legs
- 2 tablespoons olive oil
- 3 garlic cloves, minced
- 1 teaspoon dried rosemary
- 1 teaspoon dried thyme
- 1 teaspoon dried basil
- 1 teaspoon dried tarragon
- 1/3 cup water
- 1/3 cup coconut aminos
- salt and black pepper, to taste

Instructions:

1. Rub the turkey legs with olive oil.
2. Mix rosemary, thyme, basil, tarragon, salt and pepper in a bowl. Season the turkey legs with the spices.
3. Pour water and coconut aminos to the Instant Pot. Add turkey legs and garlic, close the cover, turn the vent to "Sealed".
4. Press "Manual" button, set the clock for 25 minutes and set "Strain" to high.
5. Once the clock is up, press "Drop" button and permit the strain to be delivered normally, until the float valve drops down.
6. Open the lid.
   NOTE: Make sure the tension is completely delivered prior to opening the top, so you don't get burnt.

Nutritional info:
Calories: 401
Fats (g): 36
Fiber (g): 0.5
Net carbs (g): 5
Protein (g): 24

Stuffed Turkey Breast Roast

Cooking Time: 35 minutes

Servings: 8

Ingredients:

- 3 pound turkey breast, butterflied
- 2 tablespoons organic grass-fed butter
- 2 celery stalks, chopped
- 2 red onions, chopped
- 2 garlic cloves, minced
- 2 leaves sage, fresh, chopped
- 1 ½ teaspoons salt
- a pinch of black pepper
- 2 cups flaxseed meal
- 1 cup coconut milk
- 2 tablespoons springs parsley,
- chopped 1 tablespoon olive oil
- 2 teaspoons grainy mustard
- 2 cups vegetable stock

Instructions:

1. Press "Sauté" button on the tension cooker, add oil and hotness it up.
2. Add celery, garlic and sage. Sauté for around 5 minutes with the top open till celery and onions mellow. Press "Keep warm/Cancel" button.
3. Mix flaxseed supper, a teaspoon of salt and parsley in a bowl. Blend in with a fork and pour coconut milk gradually. Mix until milk is equally spread into mixture.
4. Add cooked vegetables into the combination and blend well.
5. Pound the turkey bosom a piece to an even thickness. Season the butterflied bosom with the leftover salt and pepper.

6. Spread the vegetables and milk blend in the turkey bosom, leave some space close the edges.
7. Roll the turkey bosom firmly, utilize the cooking string or toothpicks to hold the meat edges together.
8. Press "Sauté" button on the strain cooker, add oil and hotness it up once again.
9. Put the meat to the pot and brown on all sides for around 5 minutes each. For "Keep warm/Cancel" button.
10. Add vegetable stock to the tension cooker and set grainy mustard on top of the meat, spread evenly.
11. Close the cover, and turn the vent to "Fixed". Press "Manual" button, set the clock for 25 minutes and set "Strain" to high.
12. Once the clock is up, press "Drop" button and permit the strain to be delivered normally, until the float valve drops down.
13. Open the lid.
    NOTE: Make sure the tension is completely delivered prior to opening the top, so you don't get burnt.

Nutritional info:

Calories: 198

Fats (g): 16.8

Fiber (g): 1.5

Net carbs (g):

19 Protein (g):

24.6

Garlic-Herb Turkey Breast

Cooking time: 30 minutes

Servings: 8

Ingredients:

- 4 lb turkey breast
- 2 garlic cloves, peeled

- 1 teaspoon dried rosemary
- 1 teaspoon dried thyme
- 1 cup chicken stock
- ½ teaspoon black ground pepper
- 4 tablespoons organic grass-fed butter, melted
- salt, to taste

Instructions:

1. Mix spread, rosemary, thyme and dark ground pepper in a bowl.
2. Pat the meat with paper towels to dry. Liberally rub all leaves behind salt and pepper, then, at that point, with margarine mixture.
3. Add stock to the Instant pot and the turkey bosom. Close the cover, and turn the vent to "Sealed".
4. Press "Manual" button, set the clock for 25 minutes and set "Tension" to high.
5. Once the clock is up, press "Drop" button and permit the strain to be delivered normally, until the float valve drops down.
6. Open the lid.
   NOTE: Make sure the strain is completely delivered prior to opening the top, so you don't get burnt.
7. If you like firm meat, sear it in the stove for 5-10 minutes on each side.

Nutritional info:

Calories: 387

Fats (g): 32.8

Fiber (g): 1.7

Net carbs (g): 13.4

Protein (g): 21.9

Whole Herb Stuffed Turkey

Cooking time: 50 minutes

Servings: 4

Ingredients:

- 8-10 lb whole turkey
- 2 sprigs fresh rosemary
- 2 sprigs fresh thyme
- 2 sprigs fresh sage
- 1 cup white cooking wine
- 1/3 cup flaxseed meal
- salt and pepper, to taste

Instructions:

1. Pat the turkey with paper towels to dry. Stuff the turkey with the

spices: rosemary, thyme and sage.
2. Season the turkey with salt and pepper. Put it into the Instant Pot.
3. Add wine to the pot and close the top, turn the vent to "Sealed".
4. Press "Manual" button, set the clock for 45 minutes and set "Tension" to high.
5. Once the clock is up, press "Drop" button and permit the strain to be delivered normally, until the float valve drops down.
6. Open the lid.
   NOTE: Make sure the tension is completely delivered prior to opening the top, so you don't get burnt.
7. Transfer the turkey to a plate. Press "Sauté" button on the strain cooker, add flaxseed meal.
8. Cook with the top open for 3-5 minutes mixing great. Serve the turkey with gravy.

Nutritional info:

Calories: 207

Fats (g): 19.7

Fiber (g): 2.2 Net

carbs (g): 3.6

Protein (g): 12.1

Glazed Apple Turkey Meatballs

Cooking time: 15 minutes

Servings: 3

Ingredients:

- 1 pound ground turkey
- 3 teaspoons garlic cloves, minced
- ⅛ cup applesauce
- ⅓ cup green onion scallion, sliced
- ⅓ cup almond flour

- 1 tablespoon arrowroot flour
- ⅓ cup apple, peeled, grated
- ½ teaspoon cayenne pepper
- 1 teaspoon sea salt
- 2 teaspoons cinnamon
- 1 cup apple juice
- ½ cup coconut aminos
- 1 teaspoon ginger, minced
- ¼ teaspoon black pepper
- ¼ teaspoon nutmeg, ground

Instructions:

1. Mix ground turkey, fruit purée, garlic, green onions, apples, almond flour, cayenne pepper, cinnamon, and salt in a bowl. Structure medium estimated meatballs.
2. Mix squeezed apple, ginger, coconut aminos, fruit purée, salt, arrowroot flour, nutmeg and pepper in a different bowl.
3. Put meatballs to the Instant pot and pour the squeezed apple blend on top.
4. Close the top. Press "Manual" button, set the clock for 6 minutes and set "Tension" to high.
5. Once the clock is up, press "Drop" button and permit the strain to be delivered normally, until the float valve drops down.
Open the lid.
NOTE: Make sure the tension is completely delivered prior to opening the top, so you don't get burnt.
6. Remove the meatballs from the tension cooker. Press "Sauté" button on the tension cooker.
7. Cook the sauce for 2 minutes with the cover open until thickens.

Nutritional info:

Calories: 482

Fats (g): 33.5

Fiber (g): 2.8
Net carbs (g): 16.2
Protein (g): 24.8

Grapefruit Turkey Tenderloin

Cooking time: 20 minutes
Servings: 4

Ingredients:

- 1 pound turkey tenderloin
- 1/3 cup chicken broth
- 2 tablespoons grapefruit zest
- 4 tablespoons grapefruit juice
- 1 tablespoon raw honey
- 1 teaspoon garlic powder
- 1 tablespoon cilantro
- ½ grapefruit, sliced
- salt and pepper, to taste

Instructions:

1. Season turkey with salt and pepper. Blend honey, grapefruit zing and juice, garlic powder and cilantro in a bowl.
2. Pour stock into the Instant pot. Add tenderloin.
3. Pour honey blend on top and close the cover, turn the vent to "Sealed".
4. Press "Poultry" button, set the clock for 20 minutes and set "Strain" to high.
5. Once the clock is up, press "Drop" button and permit the strain to be delivered normally, until the float valve drops down.
6. *Open the lid.*
   NOTE: Make sure the tension is completely delivered prior to opening the top, so you don't get burnt.

Nutritional info:
Calories: 144
Fats (g): 11.6
Fiber (g): 0.2 Net carbs (g): 5.5
Protein (g): 28.7

Spicy Turkey Drumsticks

Cooking time: 35 minutes
Servings: 4

Ingredients:

- 6 big turkey drumsticks
- 1 cup organic chicken
- broth 1 tablespoon ghee
- 2 carrots, chopped
- 2 celery stalks, chopped
- 2 leeks, chopped
- 2 chili peppers, seeds removed, chopped
- 2 tablespoons lime juice
- ½ teaspoon onion powder

- ½ teaspoon garlic powder
- ½ teaspoon dried oregano
- ½ teaspoon cumin
- salt and pepper, to taste

Instructions:

1. Add ghee to the Instant pot, press "Sauté" button, and hotness it up.
2. Add carrots, celery and leeks, sauté for 4-5 minutes mixing from time to time.
3. Season drumsticks with salt, pepper, onion powder, garlic powder, dried oregano and cumin.
4. Press "Keep warm/Cancel" button on the Instant pot, add turkey legs, stock, lime juice, stew peppers, more salt and pepper.
5. Close the top, and turn the vent to "Sealed".
6. Press "Manual" button, set the clock for 30 minutes and set "Tension" to high.
7. Once the clock is up press "Drop" button and turn the steam discharge handle to "Venting" position for speedy delivery, until the float valve drops down.
8. Open the lid.
   NOTE: Make sure the tension is completely delivered prior to opening the top, so you don't get burnt.

Nutritional info:

Calories: 217

Fats (g): 10.5

Fiber (g): 1.3

Net carbs (g):

7.8 Protein (g):

23.6

Turkey Frittata

Cooking time: 15 minutes

Servings: 6

Ingredients:

- 1 pound ground turkey
- 2 tablespoons almond milk 7
- eggs
- 1 onion, sliced
- 2 garlic cloves, minced 1
- tablespoon olive oil 1 cup
- fresh spinach
- 1 tablespoon lemon juice 1
- teaspoon garlic powder
- ½ teaspoon red pepper flakes 1
- cup water
- salt and pepper, to taste

Instructions:

1. Add oil to Instant Pot and press "Sauté" button.
2. Add onion and cook for 2-3 minutes until relax. Add garlic and cook for 1 more minute.
3. Add turkey and cook for 4-5 minutes until no longer pink.
4. Add spinach and cook for 2-3 additional minutes. Press "Keep warm/Cancel" button.
5. Whisk eggs and almond milk in a bowl. Add salt, pepper, lemon juice, garlic powder and red pepper flakes.
6. Grease a springform skillet with oil or cooking splash. Ensure the skillet squeezes into the Instant pot.
7. Add turkey spinach blend to the dish. Add eggs mixture.
8. Place a trivet into the Instant pot, empty water into the pot and put the skillet on the trivet.
9. Close the cover, and turn the vent to "Sealed".
10. Press "Manual" button, set the clock for 5 minutes and set "Strain" to high.

11. Once the clock is up press "Drop" button and turn the steam discharge handle to "Venting" position for speedy delivery, until the float valve drops down.
12. Open the lid.
    NOTE: Make sure the tension is completely delivered prior to opening the top, so you don't get burnt.

Nutritional info:

Calories: 265

Fats (g): 17

Fiber (g): 0.7 Net

carbs (g): 3.4

Protein (g): 27.8

Turkey Veggies Soup

Cooking time: 20 minutes

Servings: 6

Ingredients:

- 3 cups turkey meat, cooked, shredded
- 1 tablespoon olive oil
- 1 onion, chopped
- 2 carrots, chopped
- 2 celery stalks, chopped
- ½ cauliflower head, florets chopped
- 2 garlic cloves, minced
- 3 cups chicken or vegetable broth
- 1 bay leave
- salt and pepper, to taste

Instructions:

1. Add oil to Instant Pot and press "Sauté" button.
2. Add onion, carrots, garlic and celery, sauté for 4-5 minutes

blending occasionally. Press "Keep warm/Cancel" button.
3. Pour stock into the Instant pot, add turkey, vegetables, salt, pepper, cauliflower and cove leave.
4. Close the top, and turn the vent to "Sealed".
5. Press "Manual" button, set the clock for 15 minutes and set "Strain" to high.
6. Once the clock is up press "Drop" button and turn the steam discharge handle to "Venting" position for fast delivery, until the float valve drops down.
7. *Open the lid.*

   NOTE: *Make sure the tension is completely delivered prior to opening the cover, so you don't get burnt.*

Nutritional info:

Calories: 269

Fats (g): 18

Fiber (g): 1.6 Net

carbs (g): 5.5

Protein (g): 41.7

Paleo Turkey Chili

Cooking time: 30 minutes

Servings: 4

Ingredients:

- 2 tablespoons olive oil
- 1 pound ground turkey
- 1 medium sized onion, finely sliced
- 1 green bell pepper medium sized, cored and sliced 3 carrots, peeled and finely sliced
- 3 stalks celery, thinly sliced
- 3 cloves garlic, minced
- 1 can crushed tomatoes
- 1 can petite diced tomatoes
- ½ cup water

- 3 tablespoons chili powder, salt free
- 1 tablespoon dried oregano
- 1 tablespoon dried basil
- 1 teaspoon ground cumin
- 1 teaspoon onion powder
- salt and pepper, to taste

Instructions:

1. Press "Sauté" button on the strain cooker, add oil and hotness it up.
2. Add turkey and cook with the top open mixing to break meat to little pieces, for around 4 minutes till isn't pink anymore.
3. Add onion, pepper, carrots, garlic and celery, cook mixing for around 3 minutes.
4. Add tomatoes, diced tomatoes, stew powder, cumin, water, salt, oregano, basil, cumin and onion powder, mix well. Press "Keep warm/Cancel" button.
5. Close the cover, and turn the vent to "Fixed". Press "Manual" button, set the clock for 20 minutes and set "Strain" to high.
6. Once the clock is up press "Drop" button and turn the steam discharge handle to "Venting" position for speedy delivery, until the float valve drops down.
7. Open the lid.
   NOTE: Make sure the tension is completely delivered prior to opening the top, so you don't get burnt.

Nutritional info:

Calories: 364

Fats (g): 20.7

Fiber (g): 2.3

Net carbs (g): 17.2

Protein (g): 24.3

Curry Lamb Spareribs

Cooking time: 15 minutes

Servings: 4

Ingredients:

- 2.5 pounds lamb spare ribs
- 1 tablespoon curry powder
- 3 teaspoons kosher salt
- 1 yellow onion, chopped
- 1 tablespoon coconut oil
- 5 garlic cloves, minced
- ½ pound ripe tomatoes
- juice from 1 lemon
- ½ cup water
- 1 tablespoon curry powder
- 4 scallions, thinly sliced
- 1 ¼ cups cilantro, chopped and divided

Instructions:

1. Season the ribs with a tablespoon of curry powder and 2 teaspoons of salt. Utilize your hands to ensure that all parts are covered with the seasoning.
2. Put the ribs in a bowl, cover and refrigerate for something like four hours or overnight.
3. Press "Sauté" button on the tension cooker, add coconut oil and hotness it up.
4. Brown the ribs from the two sides for 2-3 minutes. Move ribs to a plate.
5. Put the tomatoes and onion into a food processor and mix until smooth.
6. Sauté garlic in the Instant pot for 1 moment. Mix in onion and tomato puree.
7. Press "Keep warm/Cancel" button. Add lemon squeeze, a cup of cleaved cilantro, curry powder and salt. Set the meat back to the pot.

Mix to cover the spareribs with the sauce, add water.
8. Close the top. Press "Manual" button, set the clock for 6 minutes and set "Strain" to high.
9. Once the clock is up, press "Drop" button and permit the strain to be delivered normally, until the float valve drops down.
10. Open the lid.
    NOTE: Make sure the tension is completely delivered prior to opening the top, so you don't get burnt.
11. Add the remainder of slashed cilantro and scallions, mix well.

Nutritional info:

Calories: 352

Fats (g): 28.8

Fiber (g): 2.4 Net

carbs (g): 8.2

Protein (g): 16.1

Sweet Maple Lamb

Cooking time: 90 minutes

Servings: 6

Ingredients:

- 2 pounds lamb leg
- 3 garlic cloves, minced
- 3 sprigs thyme
- 2 tablespoons olive oil
- ½ teaspoon dried or fresh rosemary
- 2 tablespoons Dijon mustard
- ½ cup Maple syrup
- ½ cup water
- salt, pepper, to taste

Instructions:

1. Add oil to Instant Pot and press "Sauté" button.
2. Add sheep leg and earthy colored it on each side. Season with salt and pepper.
3. Mix mustard, garlic, thyme, rosemary and Maple syrup in a bowl.
4. Add water to the Instant pot. Add sheep and pour the syrup marinade on top.
5. Close the top, and turn the vent to "Sealed".
6. Press "Manual" button, set the clock for an hour and a half and set "Tension" to high.
7. When the clock is up, press "Drop" button and permit the strain to be delivered normally, until the float valve drops down.
8. *Open the lid.*
   NOTE: Make sure the tension is completely delivered prior to opening the top, so you don't get burnt.
9. Slice the meat and present with vegetables or cauliflower rice/puree.

Nutritional info:

Calories: 371

Fats (g): 24.5

Fiber (g): 0.4 Net

carbs (g): 8.8

Protein (g): 40.3

Lamb Tomato Chops

Cooking time: 15 minutes
Servings: 4

Ingredients:

- 1 pound lamb chops
- 1 tablespoon olive
- oil 1 onion, sliced
- 2 garlic cloves,
- minced 1 teaspoon rosemary
- 1 can (14 oz) diced tomatoes
- 1 cup chicken stock
- salt, pepper, to taste

Instructions:

1. Add oil to Instant Pot and press "Sauté" button.
2. Add onion and cook for 2-3 minutes until delicate. Add garlic and cook for 1 more minute.

3. Season cleaves with salt and pepper. Add them to the Instant pot and brown on the two sides for 2-3 minutes.
4. Press "Drop" button, add stock, rosemary and tomatoes, more salt and pepper.
5. Close the cover, and turn the vent to "Sealed".
6. Press "Manual" button, set the clock for 10 minutes and set "Strain" to low.
7. Once the clock is up press "Drop" button and turn the steam discharge handle to "Venting" position for fast delivery, until the float valve drops down.
8. Open the lid.
   NOTE: Make sure the tension is completely delivered prior to opening the top, so you don't get burnt.

Nutritional info:

Calories: 268

Fats (g): 12.1

Fiber (g): 1.4 Net

carbs (g): 5.8

Protein (g): 32.9

Lamb Soup

Cooking time: 25 minutes

Servings: 4

Ingredients:

- 4 lamb shanks
- 1 onion, chopped
- 3 garlic cloves, chopped 2
- celery stalks, chopped 1
- teaspoon cumin
- 1 teaspoon thyme
- 1 teaspoon paprika

- 1 can (14 oz) tomatoes 3
- cups chicken stock
- 1 teaspoon coriander
- 1 tablespoon coconut oil
- parsley, chopped
- salt, pepper, to taste

Instructions:

1. Add oil to Instant Pot and press "Sauté" button.
2. Add onion, garlic and celery, sauté for 3-4 minutes.
3. Add legs of lamb and brown on each side for 2-3 minutes.
4. Press "Keep warm/Cancel" and add stock, tomatoes, thyme, cumin, paprika, coriander, salt and pepper.
5. Close the top, and turn the vent to "Sealed".
6. Press "Manual" button, set the clock for 20 minutes and set "Strain" to high.
7. Once the clock is up, press "Drop" button and permit the strain to be delivered normally, until the float valve drops down.
8. Open the lid.
   NOTE: Make sure the strain is completely delivered prior to opening the top, so you don't get burnt.
9. Serve finished off with hacked parsley.

Nutritional info:

Calories: 267
Fats (g): 13.7
Fiber (g): 3.7
Net carbs (g): 12.7
Protein (g): 28.2

North African Lamb Soup

Cooking time: 20 minutes
Servings: 4

Ingredients:

- 1 pound ground lamb
- 3 oz dried apricots, chopped
- 2 tablespoons olive oil
- 1 stalk celery, chopped
- 1 bell pepper, chopped
- ½ can (7 oz) diced tomatoes
- 2 garlic cloves, minced
- 2 teaspoons ground cinnamon
- 2 teaspoons ground cumin
- 2 teaspoons paprika
- 1 lemon, juiced
- 10 oz water
- 1 teaspoon erythritol
- salt, pepper, to taste

Instructions:

1. Soak apricots in water for 1-2 hours, drain.
2. Add oil to Instant Pot and press "Sauté" button.
3. Add ground sheep and cook for 2-3 minutes until somewhat brown. Press "Keep warm/Cancel" button.
4. Add apricots, celery, ringer pepper and diced tomatoes into the Instant pot.
5. Add water, lemon juice to the cooker, add garlic, ground cinnamon, ground cumin, paprika, erythritol, salt and pepper.
6. Close the top, and turn the vent to "Sealed".
7. Press "Manual" button, set the clock for 15 minutes and set "Strain" to high.
8. Once the clock is up press "Drop" button and turn the steam discharge handle to "Venting" position for speedy delivery, until the float valve drops down.

9. Open the lid.
   NOTE: Make sure the tension is completely delivered prior to opening the top, so you don't get burnt.

Nutritional info:

Calories: 313

Fats (g): 16

Fiber (g): 2.7

Net carbs (g): 11

Protein (g): 33.3

Lamb Bone Broth

Cooking time: 60 minutes

Servings: 4

Ingredients:

- 1 pound lamb bones
- 1 onion, diced
- 1 carrot, diced

- 1 stalk celery, chopped
- 2 garlic cloves, minced
- 3 sprigs rosemary
- 3 sprigs thyme
- 10 cups water
- salt, pepper, to taste

Instructions:

1. Add sheep, onion, carrot, celery, rosemary and thyme to the Instant pot.
2. Add water, salt and pepper, blend well.
3. Close the top of the Instant pot, and set vent to "Sealed".
4. Press "Manual" button, set the clock for an hour and set "Tension" to high.
5. Once the clock is up press "Drop" button and turn the steam discharge handle to "Venting" position for fast delivery, until the float valve drops down.
6. Open the lid.
   NOTE: Make sure the tension is completely delivered prior to opening the top, so you don't get burnt.
7. Set stock to the side to cool for an hour prior to taking out the solids.
8. Refrigerate for as long as 8 hours or short-term. Eliminate fat from the top if needed.

Nutritional info:

Calories: 236

Fats (g): 10.6

Fiber (g): 1.7 Net

carbs (g): 5.8

Protein (g): 32.5

Lamb Curry

Cooking time: 25 minutes

Servings: 6

Ingredients:

- 2 pounds lamb shoulder, diced 3
- teaspoons coconut oil
- 1 onion, diced
- 1 celery stalk, diced 1
- carrot, diced
- 3 garlic cloves, minced 2
- cups coconut milk
- 2 tablespoons tomato paste
- 3 teaspoons garam masala powder 2
- teaspoons turmeric powder
- 2 teaspoons ginger, chopped 2
- teaspoons ground cumin
- 2 teaspoons coriander
- 1 teaspoon ground cardamom 1
- lemon, juiced
- salt, pepper, to taste

Instructions:

1. Add 1 tablespoon oil to Instant Pot and press "Sauté" button.
2. Add sheep and cook for 2-3 minutes. Add onion, celery, carrot and garlic, mix well and cook for 2 additional minutes.
3. Add garam masala powder, turmeric powder, ginger, cumin, coriander and cardamom, cook for 1-2 additional minutes stirring constantly.
4. Press "Keep warm/Cancel" button and add coconut milk, lemon juice, tomato glue, salt and pepper.
5. Close the cover, and turn the vent to "Sealed".
6. Press "Manual" button, set the clock for 20 minutes and set

"Strain" to high.

7. Once the clock is up, press "Drop" button and permit the strain to be delivered normally, until the float valve drops down.
8. Open the lid.
   NOTE: Make sure the tension is completely delivered prior to opening the top, so you don't get burnt.

Nutritional info:

Calories: 515

Fats (g): 32.8

Fiber (g): 3.4

Net carbs (g): 11.1

Protein (g): 45.3

Middle Eastern Lamb Stew

Cooking time: 55 minutes

Servings: 6

Ingredients:

- 2 pounds lamb stew meat, cubed 2
- tablespoons olive oil
- 1 onion, diced
- 4 garlic cloves, chopped
- 2 tablespoons tomato paste
- ¼ cup apple cider vinegar 2
- tablespoons raw honey 1
- teaspoon cumin
- 1 teaspoon coriander
- 1 teaspoon turmeric
- 1 teaspoon cinnamon 1
- ½ cup chicken stock
- ¼ cup dried apricots
-

salt, pepper, to taste

Instructions:

1. Soak apricots in water for 1-2 hours, drain.
2. Add oil to Instant Pot and press "Sauté" button.
3. Add sheep and cook for 3-4 minutes until marginally brown.
4. Add onion and garlic, cook for 2 additional minutes.
5. Press "Drop" button, add stock, tomato glue, vinegar, honey, cumin, coriander, turmeric, cinnamon, apricots, salt and pepper.
6. Close the top, and turn the vent to "Sealed".
7. Press "Manual" button, set the clock for 50 minutes and set "Tension" to high.
8. Once the clock is up, press "Drop" button and permit the strain to be delivered normally, until the float valve drops down.
9. Open the lid.
   NOTE: Make sure the tension is completely delivered prior to opening the top, so you don't get burnt.
10. Serve the stew all alone or with cauliflower rice.

Nutritional info:

Calories: 368

Fats (g): 16.1

Fiber (g): 1.1

Net carbs (g): 10.8

Protein (g): 43.4

Garlic Lamb Shanks

Cooking time: 50 minutes
Servings: 6

Ingredients:

- 3 pounds lamb shanks
- 2 tablespoons Dijon mustard
- 1 ½ cup beef or chicken
- stock 1 tablespoon olive oil
- 2 onions, sliced
- 1 garlic head, peeled, minced
- 1 celery, diced
- 1 carrot, diced
- ½ cup red wine
- 1 teaspoon rosemary
-

salt, pepper, to taste

Instructions:

1. Add oil to Instant Pot and press "Sauté" button.
2. Add legs of lamb and brown on each side for 2-3 minutes.
3. Add onion, celery and carrot, cook for 3-4 additional minutes.
4. Press "Keep warm/Cancel" button, add garlic, Dijon mustard, red wine, rosemary, salt and pepper.
5. Close the top, and turn the vent to "Sealed".
6. Press "Manual" button, set the clock for 45 minutes and set "Tension" to high.
7. Once the clock is up, press "Drop" button and permit the strain to be delivered normally, until the float valve drops down.
8. Open the lid.
   NOTE: Make sure the strain is completely delivered prior to opening the top, so you don't get burnt.
9. Serve with cauliflower puree.

Nutritional info:
Calories: 504
Fats (g): 19.4
Fiber (g): 1.7 Net
carbs (g): 9.6
Protein (g): 65.9

Lamb Meatloaf

Cooking time: 20 minutes
Servings: 6

Ingredients:

- 2 pounds ground lamb
- 1 onion, chopped
- 2 garlic cloves

- 1 teaspoon cumin
- 1 teaspoon oregano
- 1 teaspoon paprika
- 1 teaspoon olive oil
- ½ cup beef broth or stock
- ½ tablespoon tomato paste
- salt, pepper, to taste

Instructions:

1. Add onion and garlic to a blender and heartbeat for 2-3 times. Add sheep meat, salt, pepper, cumin, oregano and paprika, mix until smooth.
2. Mold the blend into a meatloaf shape that will impeccably squeeze into Instant Pot.
3. Add oil into Instant Pot and press "Sauté" button.
4. Add portion and brown on each side for 2-3 minutes. Press "Keep warm/Cancel" button, add stock and tomato paste.
5. Close the cover, and turn the vent to "Sealed".
6. Press "Manual" button, set the clock for 15 minutes and set "Strain" to high.
7. Once the clock is up, press "Drop" button and permit the strain to be delivered normally, until the float valve drops down.
8. Open the lid.
   NOTE: Make sure the tension is completely delivered prior to opening the top, so you don't get burnt.

Nutritional info:

Calories: 304

Fats (g): 12.2

Fiber (g): 0.7 Net

carbs (g): 2.9

Protein (g): 43.3

Lamb Burgers with Caramelized Onion

Cooking time: 35 minutes

Servings: 4

Ingredients:

- 2 onions, sliced
- 1 onion, chopped
- 2 tablespoons olive oil
- 1 ½ pound ground
- lamb 1 teaspoon cloves
- 1 teaspoon cumin
- 1 teaspoon red pepper
- flakes 1 cup water
- salt, pepper, to taste

Instructions:

1. Add oil to Instant Pot and press "Sauté" button.
2. Add cut onion, add salt and cook for 20-25 minutes mixing every now and then, until the onion is caramelized. Press "Keep warm/Cancel" button. Move onion to a plate.
3. Mix ground sheep, cleaved onion, cloves, salt, pepper, cumin and red pepper flakes.
4. Form round patties, add a few more oil to the Instant pot and press "Sauté" button.
5. Add patties to the Instant pot and cook them for 3-4 minutes on each side.
6. Add water to the Instant pot and spot a rack inside. Set patties on the rack.
7. Close the cover, and turn the vent to "Sealed".
8. Press "Manual" button, set the clock for 13 minutes and set "Tension" to high.
9. Once the clock is up press "Drop" button and turn the steam discharge handle to "Venting" position for fast delivery, until the float valve drops down.

10. Open the lid.
    NOTE: Make sure the strain is completely delivered prior to opening the top, so you don't get burnt.
11. Serve patties on lettuce or paleo buns with caramelized onion.

Nutritional info:

Calories: 415

Fats (g): 19.9

Fiber (g): 2.1 Net

carbs (g): 8.5

Protein (g): 48.8

Moroccan Lamb Chops

Cooking time: 15 minutes

Servings: 6

Ingredients:

- 2 ½ pounds lamb chops
- 2 tablespoons Moroccan spice mix (Ras el Hanout)
- 1 cup beef stock
- ¼ cup olive oil

- 2 tablespoons lemon juice
- ¼ cup fresh parsley, chopped
- 2 tablespoons fresh mint, chopped
- ½ teaspoon smoked paprika
- 1 teaspoon red pepper flakes 3 garlic cloves, chopped
- 2 tablespoons lemon zest
- salt, pepper, to taste

Instructions:

1. Season cleaves with salt and pepper.
2. Add 1 tablespoon oil to Instant Pot and press "Sauté" button.
3. Add hacks to the Instant pot and brown on the two sides for 2-3 minutes.
4. Press "Keep warm/Cancel" button, add stock and Moroccan zest blend to the Instant pot.
5. Close the top, and turn the vent to "Sealed".
6. Press "Manual" button, set the clock for 10 minutes and set "Tension" to low.
7. Once the clock is up press "Drop" button and turn the steam discharge handle to "Venting" position for speedy delivery, until the float valve drops down.
8. Open the lid.
   NOTE: Make sure the strain is completely delivered prior to opening the top, so you don't get burnt.
9. Blend the elements for the Charmoula sauce: oil, lemon juice, parsley, new mint, smoked paprika, pepper chips, garlic, lemon zing, salt and pepper. The sauce should look like pesto.
10. Serve sheep slashes with the Charmoula sauce.

Nutritional info:

Calories: 651

Fats (g): 33.8
Fiber (g): 0.8 Net
carbs (g): 2.4
Protein (g): 60.9

Rack of Lamb

Cooking time: 95 minutes

Servings: 8

Ingredients:

- 2 pounds rack lamb
- 3 tablespoons olive oil
- 1 cup red wine
- 2 tablespoons fresh rosemary
- 1 tablespoon fresh thyme
- 3 garlic cloves, minced
- 1 teaspoon lemon zest
- 1 teaspoon ginger, minced
- 1 cup beef stock
- salt, pepper, to taste

Instructions:

1. Add oil to Instant Pot and press "Sauté" button. Earthy colored rack sheep on each side for 2-3 minutes. Press "Keep warm/Cancel" button.
2. Mix red wine, rosemary, thyme, garlic, lemon zing, ginger, salt and pepper in a bowl.
3. Add water to the Instant pot; pour the wine combination on top of the sheep rack.
4. Close the cover, and turn the vent to "Sealed".
5. Press "Manual" button, set the clock for an hour and a half and set "Strain" to high.

6. Once the clock is up, press "Drop" button and permit the strain to be delivered normally, until the float valve drops down.
7. Open the lid.
   NOTE: Make sure the tension is completely delivered prior to opening the top, so you don't get burnt.
8. Serve with juices from your Instant pot and vegetables on the side.

Nutritional info:

Calories: 268

Fats (g): 15.5

Fiber (g): 0.6 Net

carbs (g): 2.1

Protein (g): 23.5

Lamb Liver with Grapes

Cooking time: 15 minutes

Servings: 6

Ingredients:

- 2 lamb livers
- 1 tablespoon olive oil
- 1 onion, sliced
- 3 oz black grapes, halved
- 1 teaspoon grape juice
- 1 tablespoon lemon juice
- 1 teaspoon hot sauce
- 2 cups water
- salt, pepper, to taste

Instructions:

1. Season the liver with salt and pepper. Add oil to Instant Pot and press "Sauté" button.

2. Add liver to the Instant pot and cook on each side for 2 minutes. Move to a plate.
3. Add some more oil to the cooker, add onion and cook for 2-3 minutes. Add grapes and cook for 1 more minute.
4. Add grape juice, lemon juice and hot sauce, cook for 2-3 additional minutes blending constantly.
5. Press "Keep warm/Cancel" button, add liver to the Instant pot, add water, more salt and pepper.
6. Close the top, and turn the vent to "Sealed".
7. Press "Meat/Stew" button, set the clock for 10 minutes and set "Strain" to high.
8. Once the clock is up press "Drop" button and turn the steam discharge handle to "Venting" position for speedy delivery, until the float valve drops down.
9. Open the lid.
   NOTE: Make sure the tension is completely delivered prior to opening the cover, so you don't get burnt.
10. Slice the liver and present with sauce from the cooker.

Nutritional info:

Calories: 301

Fats (g): 24.6

Fiber (g): 1.2 Net

carbs (g): 6.1

Protein (g): 26.4

Original Lamb Stew

Cooking time: 15 minutes

Servings: 4

Ingredients:

- 1 pound lamb stew meat, cut into small pieces
- 1 onion, sliced
- 1 cup water
- 1 cup carrots, baby-cut
- ¼ teaspoon black pepper
- 1 garlic clove, minced
- 1 teaspoon salt
- 1 tablespoon arrowroot starch, dissolved in ¼ cup cold water
- 1 tablespoon Worcestershire sauce

Instructions:

1. Press "Sauté" button on the tension cooker, add garlic, onion, water, Worcestershire sauce and sheep meat, cook for 3-4 minutes mixing constantly.
2. Press "Keep warm/Cancel" button. Close the cover, and turn the vent to "Sealed".
3. Press "Manual" button, set the clock for 10 minutes and set "Tension" to high.
4. Once the clock is up press "Drop" button and turn the steam discharge handle to "Venting" position for fast delivery, until the float valve drops down.
5. Open the lid.
   NOTE: Make sure the strain is completely delivered prior to opening the top, so you don't get burnt.
6. Add carrots, season with salt and pepper. Close the top. Press "Manual" button, set the clock for 10 minutes and set "Strain" to high.
7. Once the clock is up press "Drop" button and turn the steam discharge handle to "Venting" position for fast delivery, until the float valve drops down. Open the lid.
8. Remove the meat from the tension cooker. Add the broke down arrowroot starch and mix until the sauce thickens.
9. Serve the meat with the sauce from the cooker.

Nutritional info:

Calories: 315

Fats (g): 18.8

Fiber (g): 1.3 Net

carbs (g): 6.4

Protein (g): 26.8

Classic Beef Stew

Cooking time: 15 minutes

Servings: 8

Ingredients:

- 3 pounds beef chuck roast, cut into small pieces 2
- teaspoons olive oil
- 1 bay leaf
- salt and pepper, to taste
- 2 garlic cloves, finely chopped 1
- carrot, finely chopped
- 1 onion, finely chopped
- 1 celery stalk, finely chopped 1
- tablespoon almond flour
- 2 cups baby-cut carrots
- 2 tablespoons tomato paste 1
- cup dry red wine
- 1 tablespoon organic grass-fed butter
- ¾ cup beef broth

Instructions:

1. Season the meat liberally with salt and pepper.
2. Press "Sauté" button on the strain cooker, add oil and hotness it up. Sauté the meat until brown. Move the cooked meat to a plate.
3. Add onions to the Instant Pot and cook for 2 minutes.
4. Add the celery and finely hacked carrots. Cook for 3 minutes.
5. Add hacked garlic and cook for one more moment. Add red wine and permit to cook until the fluid is decreased by half.
6. Add tomato glue and mix. Press "Keep warm/Cancel" button, add hamburger stock, cooked meat and narrows leaf.
10. Close the cover, and turn the vent to "Fixed". Press "Manual" button, set the clock for 12 minutes and set "Tension" to high.
11. Once the clock is up press "Drop" button and turn the steam discharge handle to "Venting" position for fast delivery, until the float valve drops down.

12. Open the lid.
    NOTE: Make sure the strain is completely delivered prior to opening the top, so you don't get burnt.
13. Add child slice carrots to the pot and close the lid.
14. Press "Manual" button, set the clock for 8 minutes and set "Strain" to high.
15. Once the clock is up press "Drop" button and turn the steam discharge handle to "Venting" position for speedy delivery, until the float valve drops down. Open the lid.
16. Remove the meat and carrots from the tension cooker. To make the sauce thicker, mix in the mix of spread and flour. Set back the carrots and meat to the pot when the fluid becomes thicker. Season to taste.

Nutritional info:

Calories: 593

Fats (g): 40.5

Fiber (g): 1.4

Net carbs (g): 6

Protein (g): 35.7

Ground Beef and Cabbage

Cooking time: 20 minutes

Servings: 4

Ingredients:

- 1 small cabbage, chopped
- 1 lb ground beef
- 1 onion, chopped
- 2 garlic cloves, minced
- 1 can plain diced tomatoes
- 8 oz homemade tomato sauce
- 1 tablespoon olive oil
- salt and pepper, to taste

Instructions:

1. Press "Sauté" button on the tension cooker, add oil and hotness it up.
2. Add onion and garlic for 1-2 minutes until soften.
3. Add ground hamburger and sauté until brown with the top open.
4. Add cabbage, tomato glue and pureed tomatoes. Add salt and pepper. Press "Keep warm/Cancel" button.
5. Close the cover, and turn the vent to "Fixed". Press "Manual" button, set the clock for 15 minutes and set "Tension" to high.
6. Once the clock is up, press "Drop" button and permit the strain to be delivered normally, until the float valve drops down.
7. Open the lid.
   NOTE: Make sure the strain is completely delivered prior to opening the cover, so you don't get burnt.

Nutritional info:
Calories: 251
Fats (g): 27
Fiber (g): 0.2 Net
carbs (g): 9
Protein (g): 15

Carne Guisada

Cooking time: 40 minutes

Servings: 4

Ingredients:

- 1 pound beef stew
- meat 2 tablespoons
- olive oil 1 bay leaf
- 1 tablespoon garlic, minced
- 1 onion, diced
- 1 teaspoon paprika
- 1 teaspoon ground
- cumin salt and pepper,
- to taste 1 teaspoon chili powder
- 1 serrano peppers, minced
-

1 cup broth, chicken or

beef 1 tablespoon agar agar

- 1/2 teaspoon oregano
- 1 teaspoon chipotle powder
- 1/2 cup organic (better homemade) tomato sauce

Instructions:

1. Press "Sauté" button on the strain cooker, add oil and hotness it up.
2. Add the meat and sauté it on all sides till light brown, with the top open.
3. Add onion, inlet leaf, paprika, ground cumin, stew powder, salt and pepper, oregano, chipotle powder, serrano pepper and garlic.
4. Cook for 3 additional minutes with the top open blending regularly. Press "Keep warm/Cancel" button.
5. Add pureed tomatoes and stock. Close the lid.
6. Press "Meat/Stew" button, set the clock for 35 minutes, the strain will be set automatically.
7. Once the clock is up, press "Drop" button and permit the strain to be delivered normally, until the float valve drops down.
8. Open the lid.
   NOTE: Make sure the tension is completely delivered prior to opening the top, so you don't get burnt.
9. Add some fluid from the pot to the agar to break up. Add the combination to the pot and blend well.

Nutritional info:

Calories: 491

Fats (g): 48.4

Fiber (g): 0.7

Net carbs (g): 2.7

Protein (g): 36.8

Mediterranean Beef Brisket

Cooking time: 45 minutes

Servings: 6

Ingredients:

- 1 (2-3 pound) beef brisket
- ½ pound onion, peeled and sliced
- 3 garlic cloves, peeled and chopped
- 1 teaspoon freshly ground pepper
- 1 teaspoon kosher salt
- 12 ounces white button mushrooms, rinsed and halved
- 1 teaspoon basil
- 1 teaspoon thyme
- 1 tablespoon extra virgin olive oil
- ½ pound baby-cut carrots
- 1 (15 ounce) can diced tomatoes, drained
- ½ cup beef broth

Instructions:

1. Pat the meat with a paper towel. Season all sides with salt and pepper.
2. Press "Sauté" button on the strain cooker, add oil and hotness it up.
3. Add the meat and cook with the top open on all sides until brown. Move the meat to a plate.
4. Add garlic and onion to the Instant pot and cook for 5 minutes with the cover open. Add stock and depleted tomatoes. Cook for 5 additional minutes while continually mixing. Press "Keep warm/Cancel" button.
5. Put the meat back to the pot. Put the carrots on top of the meat. Close the lid.
6. Press "Manual" button, set the clock for 35 minutes and set "Tension" to high.
7. Once the clock is up, press "Drop" button and permit the strain to be delivered normally, until the float valve drops down.

8. Open the lid.

NOTE: Make sure the tension is completely delivered prior to opening the top, so you don't get burnt.

9. Transfer the meat and veggies to a platter. Cover with foil and permit resting for 10 minutes. Daintily cut the brisket and present with veggies and sauce.

Nutritional info:

Calories: 418

Fats (g): 34.7

Fiber (g): 3

Net carbs (g): 11.1

Protein (g): 49.1

Beef Filled Lettuce Wraps

Cooking time: 25 minutes

Servings: 4

Ingredients:

- 1 lb ground beef
- 2 teaspoons olive oil
- 2 scallions, chopped
- 2 inch piece ginger, grated
- ¼ cup chopped peanuts
- 2 cloves garlic, minced
- 1 teaspoon red pepper flakes
- 1 tablespoon sriracha sauce
- 2 tablespoons coconut aminos
- ½ cup water
- salt and freshly ground black pepper, to taste
- 1 head lettuce leaves, separated, cleaned and dried

Instructions:

1. Add oil to Instant Pot and press "Sauté" button.
2. Add meat and cook for 4-5 minutes until brown. Press "Keep warm/Cancel" button.
3. Add scallions, ginger, red pepper chips, sriracha sauce, coconut aminos, salt, pepper and water to the Instant pot.
4. Close the cover, and turn the vent to "Sealed".
5. Press "Manual" button, set the clock for 20 minutes and set "Strain" to high.
6. Once the clock is up, press "Drop" button and permit the strain to be delivered normally, until the float valve drops down.
7. Open the lid.
   NOTE: Make sure the tension is completely delivered prior to opening the top, so you don't get burnt.
8. Once cooked add peanuts and season with more pepper and salt if needed.
9. Serve enclosed by lettuce leaves.

Nutritional info:

Calories: 355

Fats (g): 24.2

Fiber (g): 1.7

Net carbs (g): 16.1

Protein (g): 37.9

Beef Meatballs

Cooking time: 10 minutes

Servings: 5

Ingredients:

- 2 pounds ground
- beef 2 eggs
- 1 tablespoon olive oil
- 2 teaspoons Italian
- seasoning 1 teaspoon basil
- 1 teaspoon onion powder
- 1 teaspoon garlic powder
- ½ teaspoon red pepper flakes
- ½ teaspoon paprika
- ¼ cup coconut flour
- 2 cups tomato sauce

- 1 can (14 oz) diced tomatoes
- 1 cup water
- salt, pepper, to taste

Instructions:

1. Mix ground meat, eggs, flour, Italian flavoring, basil, onion powder, garlic powder, red pepper pieces, paprika, salt and pepper in a bowl until well combined.
2. Mold the blend into meatballs.
3. Add olive oil into Instant Pot, then, at that point, put meatballs and press "Sauté" button to brown meatballs evenly.
4. Add pureed tomatoes, tomatoes and water to the Instant pot.
5. Close the top, and turn the vent to "Sealed".
6. Press "Manual" button, set the clock for 10 minutes and set "Tension" to low.
7. Once the clock is up press "Drop" button and turn the steam discharge handle to "Venting" position for speedy delivery, until the float valve drops down.
8. Open the lid.
   NOTE: Make sure the strain is completely delivered prior to opening the top, so you don't get burnt.

Nutritional info:

Calories: 411

Fats (g): 15.2

Fiber (g): 6.7

Net carbs (g): 12.5

Protein (g): 41

Classic Beef Meatloaf

Cooking time: 38 minutes

Servings: 8

Ingredients:

- 3 pounds ground beef
- 1 egg
- 1 onion, chopped
- 2 garlic cloves, minced
- ½ cup almond flour
- 1 cup tomato sauce
- ½ teaspoon Italian seasoning
- ½ teaspoon paprika
- 1 tablespoon olive oil
- salt, pepper, to taste

Instructions:

1. Mix all fixings (without oil) in a blending bowl. Shape the combination into a type of a loaf.
2. Add olive oil into Instant Pot, add meatloaf and press "Sauté" button to brown the meat marginally. Cook meatloaf for 2-3 minutes on each side.
3. Close the cover, and turn the vent to "Sealed".
4. Press "Meat/Stew" button, set the clock for 35 minutes and set "Tension" to low.
5. When the clock is up press "Drop" button and turn the steam discharge handle to "Venting" position for fast delivery, until the float valve drops down.
6. Open the lid.
   NOTE: Make sure the tension is completely delivered prior to opening the cover, so you don't get burnt.

Nutritional info:

Calories: 364

Fats (g): 14

Fiber (g): 1

Net carbs (g): 3.7

Protein (g): 53.3

Beef Soup

Cooking time: 25 minutes

Servings: 6

Ingredients:

- 1 pound beef stew meat, cubed
- 3 carrots, diced
- 1 onion, diced
- 2 garlic cloves, chopped
- 2 tablespoons tomato paste
- 2 tablespoons olive oil
- 2 bay leaves
- 1 teaspoon almond flour
- 1 teaspoon paprika
- 1 teaspoon thyme
- 1 cup green beans
- 2 cups kale,
- chopped 6 cups beef
- broth salt, pepper, to taste

Instructions:

1. Add oil to Instant Pot and press "Sauté" button. Add meat and cook for 3-4 minutes until brown, add salt and pepper.
2. Add carrots, onion and garlic. Blend and cook for 3 additional minutes.
3. Add tomato glue, 1 cup stock and almond flour, singe for 1-2 minutes. Press "Keep warm/Cancel" button.
4. Add the leftover meat stock, cove leaves, paprika, thyme, more salt

and pepper.
5. Close the top, and turn the vent to "Sealed".
6. Press "Manual" button, set the clock for 15 minutes and set "Strain" to high.
7. Once the clock is up press "Drop" button and turn the steam discharge handle to "Venting" position for speedy delivery, until the float valve drops down.
8. *Open the lid.*
   NOTE: Make sure the tension is completely delivered prior to opening the top, so you don't get burnt.
9. Press "Sauté" button and add kale and green beans to the Instant pot. Cook for 5 minutes blending every once in a while. Press "Keep warm/Cancel" and serve.

Nutritional info:

Calories: 290

Fats (g): 23.3

Fiber (g): 3.1

Net carbs (g): 11.1

Protein (g): 30.6

Beef Curry

Cooking time: 40 minutes

Servings: 6

Ingredients:

- 2 pounds beef stew meat, cubed
- 1 onion, chopped
- 1 carrot, cubed
- 2 garlic cloves, chopped
- 1 tablespoon coconut oil
- 1 tablespoon ginger,
- chopped 3 tablespoons curry
- powder 1 cup coconut milk
- 2 tablespoons fresh coriander, chopped
- salt, pepper, to taste

Instructions:

1. Add oil to Instant Pot and press "Sauté" button. Add hamburger, salt, pepper and cook for 2-3 minutes until brown.
2. Add onion, carrot, garlic, ginger, coconut milk, curry powder, coriander, salt and pepper.
3. Close the cover, and turn the vent to "Sealed".
4. Press "Manual" button, set the clock for 35 minutes and set "Tension" to high.
5. Once the clock is up press "Drop" button and turn the steam discharge handle to "Venting" position for speedy delivery, until the float valve drops down.
6. Open the lid.
   NOTE: Make sure the strain is completely delivered prior to opening the top, so you don't get burnt.

Nutritional info:
Calories: 419
Fats (g): 21.8
Fiber (g): 2.7 Net
carbs (g): 7.7
Protein (g): 47.6

Beef Habanero Chili

Cooking time: 30 minutes
Servings: 6

Ingredients:

- 1 pound ground beef
- 1 onion, diced
- 1 bell pepper, chopped
- 2 habaneros, chopped
- 1 carrot, chopped
- 2 celery stalks, chopped
-

- 2 garlic cloves,
- 1 tablespoon olive oil
- 2 cans (14 oz) diced tomatoes
- 1 teaspoon chili powder
- 1 teaspoon paprika
- 1 teaspoon cumin
- 1 cup beef broth
- salt, pepper, to taste

Instructions:

1. Add oil to Instant Pot and press "Sauté" button. Add onion and cook for 2-3 minutes until soft.
2. Add garlic and ground hamburger, cook until the meat is brown.
3. Press "Keep warm/Cancel" and add stock, chime pepper, habaneros, carrot, celery, diced tomatoes, bean stew powder, paprika, cumin, salt and pepper.
4. Close the cover, and turn the vent to "Sealed".
5. Press "Manual" button, set the clock for 25 minutes and set "Strain" to high.
6. Once the clock is up, press "Drop" button and permit the strain to be delivered normally, until the float valve drops down.
7. Open the lid.
   NOTE: Make sure the tension is completely delivered prior to opening the top, so you don't get burnt.

Nutritional info:

Calories: 208

Fats (g): 17.7

Fiber (g): 2.2 Net

carbs (g): 9.3

Protein (g): 25.3

Paleo Tacos

Cooking time: 25 minutes

Servings: 4

Ingredients:

- 1 pound ground beef
- 1 onion, diced
- 1 bell pepper, diced
- 1 jalapeno, seeded, diced
- 2 tomatoes, diced
- 2 garlic cloves, minced
- 1 tablespoon coconut oil
- ½ teaspoon paprika
- ½ teaspoon cumin
- ½ teaspoon oregano
- ½ cup water
- salt, pepper, to taste

Instructions:

1. Add oil to Instant Pot and press "Sauté" button. Add onion and cook for 2-3 minutes until translucent.
2. Add ground hamburger, cook until the meat is brown.
3. Press "Keep warm/Cancel" and add water, chime pepper, jalapeno, tomatoes, garlic, paprika, cumin, oregano, salt and pepper.
4. Close the cover, and turn the vent to "Sealed".
5. Press "Manual" button, set the clock for 20 minutes and set "Strain" to high.
6. Once the clock is up, press "Drop" button and permit the strain to be delivered normally, until the float valve drops down.
7. Open the lid.
   NOTE: Make sure the tension is completely delivered prior to opening the top, so you don't get burnt.

8. Serve on taco shells or lettuce with your favored sauce.

Nutritional info:
Calories: 277
Fats (g): 10.8
Fiber (g): 2.1 Net
carbs (g): 8.3
Protein (g): 35.8

Beef Country Steak

Cooking time: 35 minutes
Servings: 4

Ingredients:

- 1 ½ pound beef steak meat
- 3 garlic cloves, chopped
- 1 cup beef broth
- 1 tablespoon olive oil
- 1 onion, diced,
- 1 celery stalk, diced
- ½ teaspoon cumin

- ½ teaspoon chili powder
- ¼ teaspoon oregano
- ¼ teaspoon paprika
- 2 teaspoons Worcestershire sauce
- ¼ cup almond flour
- salt, pepper, to taste

Instructions:

1. Add oil to Instant Pot and press "Sauté" button. Pat the steak with flour on the two sides, put into the Instant pot.
2. Brown steak on each side for 2-3 minutes. Press "Keep warm/Cancel" and add onion, celery, garlic, cumin, stew powder, oregano, paprika, Worcestershire sauce, stock, salt and pepper.
3. Close the top, and turn the vent to "Sealed".
4. Press "Manual" button, set the clock for 30 minutes and set "Strain" to high.
5. Once the clock is up, press "Drop" button and permit the strain to be delivered normally, until the float valve drops down.
6. Open the lid.
   NOTE: Make sure the tension is completely delivered prior to opening the cover, so you don't get burnt.

Nutritional info:

Calories: 315

Fats (g): 21.9

Fiber (g): 1.1

Net carbs (g): 5

Protein (g): 23.7

Beef Stuffed Zucchini

Cooking time: 10 minutes

Servings: 4

Ingredients:

- 4 zucchinis cut in half lengthwise
- 1 tablespoon olive oil
- 1/3 pound ground beef
- 1 onion, diced
- 2 tomatoes, diced
- 1 tablespoon tomato paste
- 2 garlic cloves, minced
- 1 teaspoon paprika
- 1 teaspoon cumin
- 1 cup water
- 1 tablespoon fresh parsley, chopped
- salt, pepper, to taste

Instructions:

1. Add oil to Instant Pot and press "Sauté" button. Add onion and cook for 1-2 minutes until soft.
2. Add ground hamburger and garlic, cook until the meat is brown. Add diced tomatoes, salt, pepper, paprika and cumin and cook for 2-3 additional minutes. Add tomato glue and mix well. Press "Keep warm/Cancel" button.
3. Remove the meat from the cooker, utilize a paper towel to clean the base. Add water to the Instant pot and supplement a trivet.
4. Stuff zucchinis with the cooked meat and vegetables. Put stuffed zucchinis on the trivet.
5. Close the top, and turn the vent to "Sealed".
6. Press "Manual" button, set the clock for 3 minutes and set "Strain" to high.
7. Once the clock is up press "Drop" button and turn the steam discharge handle to "Venting" position for speedy delivery, until the float valve drops down.
8. Open the lid.
   NOTE: Make sure the tension is completely delivered prior to opening the cover, so you don't get burnt.

9. Serve finished off with parsley.

Nutritional info:

Calories: 163

Fats (g): 16.6

Fiber (g): 3

Net carbs (g): 8.4

Protein (g): 25.2

Paleo Corned Beef

Cooking time: 50 minutes

Servings: 5

Ingredients:

- 3 pounds corned beef
- 3 bay leaves
- 2 cups water
- 1 tablespoon garlic powder
- salt, pepper, to taste

Instructions:

1. Rub all sides of the meat with garlic powder. Season with salt and pepper.
2. Add 2 cups of water to the Instant pot. For the trivet into the pot and set the carefully prepared meat on top.
3. Put the inlet leaves on top of the hamburger. Close the lid.
4. Press "Manual" button, set the clock for 50 minutes and set "Tension" to high.
5. Once the clock is up, press "Drop" button and permit the strain to be delivered normally, until the float valve drops down.
6. Open the lid.

NOTE: Make sure the strain is completely delivered prior to opening the cover, so you don't get burnt.

7. Discard the inlet leaves before serving.

Nutritional info:
Calories: 470
Fats (g): 34.1
Fiber (g): 0.4 Net
carbs (g): 1.8
Protein (g): 36.8

Pumpkin Beef Stew

Cooking time: 40 minutes

Servings: 4

Ingredients:

- ½ pound beef stew meat, cubed
- 7 oz pumpkin puree

- 2 cups beef broth
- 1 can (14 oz) diced tomatoes
- 3 tablespoons coconut oil
- ½ teaspoon rosemary
- ½ teaspoon cumin
- ½ teaspoon thyme
- salt, pepper, to taste

Instructions:

1. Add oil to Instant Pot and press "Sauté" button. Add hamburger, cook until brown.
2. Press "Keep warm/Cancel" and add stock, pumpkin puree, diced tomatoes, rosemary, cumin, thyme, salt and pepper.
3. Close the top, and turn the vent to "Sealed".
4. Press "Manual" button, set the clock for 35 minutes and set "Tension" to high.
5. Once the clock is up, press "Drop" button and permit the strain to be delivered normally, until the float valve drops down.
6. Open the lid.
NOTE: *Make sure the tension is completely delivered prior to opening the cover, so you don't get burnt.*

Nutritional info:

Calories: 241

Fats (g): 14.8

Fiber (g): 2.2

Net carbs (g): 7

Protein (g): 20.7

Beef Stroganoff

Cooking time: 30 minutes

Servings: 4

Ingredients:

- 1 pound beef stew meat, chopped
- 6 oz portabello mushrooms
- 1 can full fat coconut milk
- 1 onion, diced
- 2 garlic cloves, chopped
- ½ teaspoon cayenne
- ½ teaspoon dried parsley
- ½ teaspoon garlic powder
- ½ teaspoon onion powder
- 1 tablespoon Worcestershire sauce
- 2 cup beef broth
- salt, pepper, to taste

Instructions:

1. Refrigerate coconut milk for the time being to get coconut cream.
2. Mix salt, pepper, cayenne, parsley, garlic powder and onion powder in a bowl. Season meat with the flavor mixture.
3. Add oil to Instant Pot and press "Sauté" button. Add meat and cook for 3-4 minutes until brown. Move meat to a plate.
4. Add more oil to the Instant pot, add onion and mushrooms, cook for 5-7 minutes mixing constantly.
5. Add garlic and cook for 1 more moment. Add ½ cup stock to the cooker and scratch the earthy colored pieces off the base. Press "Keep warm/Cancel" button.
6. Add hamburger and the excess stock, Worcestershire sauce, more salt and pepper and close the cover, and turn the vent to "Sealed".
7. Press "Manual" button, set the clock for 13 minutes and set "Tension" to high.
8. Once the clock is up, press "Drop" button and permit the strain to be delivered normally, until the float valve drops down.
9. Open the lid.
   NOTE: Make sure the tension is completely delivered prior to opening

the top, so you don't get burnt.

10. Press "Sauté" button and add coconut cream to the Instant pot. Blend well and cook for 4-5 minutes. Add seriously preparing if needed.

Nutritional info:

Calories: 291

Fats (g): 10.9

Fiber (g): 1.4 Net

carbs (g): 7.6

Protein (g): 38.7

BBQ Pulled Pork

Cooking time: 90 minutes

Servings: 6

Ingredients:

- 4 pounds bone-in pork shoulder
- sea salt, pepper, to taste
- 1 teaspoon garlic powder
- 1 teaspoon onion powder
- 1 teaspoon chili powder
- 2 cups chicken stock or beef broth

For Paleo BBQ sauce (1 cup):

- 1 cup organic tomato sauce
- ½ cup chicken bone broth or water
- ½ cup apple cider vinegar
- 1/3 cup raw honey
- 2 teaspoons paprika
- ½ teaspoon onion powder
- 1 teaspoon Dijon mustard
-

salt and pepper, to taste

Instructions:

1. To make BBQ sauce, just blend every one of the fixings in a pan, heat to the point of boiling and stew for 30 minutes.
2. Mix garlic powder, onion powder, stew powder, salt and pepper in a bowl.
3. Cut the meat into more modest pieces. Rub them with the spices.
4. Put the meat to the strain cooker skin side up. Add stock or stock, close the lid.
5. Press "Manual" button, set the clock for an hour and a half and set "Strain" to high.
6. Once the clock is up, press "Drop" button and permit the strain to be delivered normally, until the float valve drops down.
7. Open the lid.

NOTE: Make sure the tension is completely delivered prior to opening the top, so you don't get burnt.

8. Put the meat on a plate or cutting load up and shred it. Serve finished off with the sauce.

Nutritional info:

Calories: 165

Fats (g): 18.3

Fiber (g): 0.7

Net carbs (g): 9

Protein (g): 12.9

Sweet Lime Ginger Pork

Cooking time: 30 minutes
Servings: 6

Ingredients:

- 2 lbs pork loin
- 1 tablespoon olive oil
- ¼ cup raw honey
- 1 tablespoon Worcestershire
- Sauce 1 lime, juiced
- 2 garlic cloves, minced
- 1 teaspoon fresh ginger, grounded
- 2 tablespoons agar agar
- 1 cup water
- salt, pepper, to taste

Instructions:

1. Add oil to Instant Pot and press "Sauté" button. For pork with salt and pepper, then, at that point, set it on the hot skillet. Cook for 2-5 minutes the two sides. Press "Keep warm/Cancel" button.
2. Mix honey, Worcestershire sauce, lime juice, garlic cloves and ginger in a bowl.
3. Pour the blend over pork, add water. Close the cover, and turn the vent to "Sealed".
4. Press "Manual" button, set the clock for 20 minutes and set "Tension" to high.
5. Once the clock is up press "Drop" button and turn the steam discharge handle to "Venting" position for fast delivery, until the float valve drops down.
6. Open the lid.
   NOTE: Make sure the strain is completely delivered prior to opening the top, so you don't get burnt.
7. Transfer the pork to a plate and press "Sauté" button on the Instant pot.
8. Add agar to the cooker. Mix until the sauce thickens. Pour over the pork and serve.

Nutritional info:

Calories: 437

Fats (g): 23.4

Fiber (g): 0.7

Net carbs (g): 10.2

Protein (g): 41.5

Green Chili Pork Stew

Cooking time: 26 minutes

Servings: 6

Ingredients:

- 1 pound pork ribs, bone-in
- 2 tablespoon coconut oil

- 2 onions, chopped
- 1 carrot, chopped
- 2 garlic cloves, chopped
- 1 can green chilis, diced
- 1 tablespoon apple cider vinegar
- 1 tablespoon raw honey
- 2 cups beef broth
- salt, pepper, to taste

Instructions:

1. Season pork ribs with salt and pepper. Add oil to Instant Pot and press "Sauté" button.
2. Add onions and garlic, cook for 2-3 minutes mixing constantly.
3. Add pork ribs and cook for 3-4 additional minutes until marginally brown. Press "Keep warm/Cancel" buttonю
4. Add stock, carrot, green stews, apple juice vinegar, honey, salt and pepper.
5. Close the cover, and turn the vent to "Sealed".
6. Press "Meat/Stew" button, set the clock for 20 minutes and set "Tension" to high.
7. Once the clock is up press "Drop" button and turn the steam discharge handle to "Venting" position for fast delivery, until the float valve

    drops down.
8. *Open the lid.*
    NOTE: Make sure the strain is completely delivered prior to opening the top, so you don't get burnt.

Nutritional info:

Calories: 442

Fats (g): 27.7

Fiber (g): 2.2

Net carbs (g): 13.6

Protein (g): 33.6

Curry Pork Stir Fry

Cooking time: 20 minutes

Servings: 6

Ingredients:

- 2 pounds pork loin, cubed
- 1 cup coconut milk
- 2 bell peppers, sliced
- 1 onion, sliced
- 2 garlic cloves, minced
- 1 tablespoon curry powder
- 1 tablespoon Sriracha sauce
- 1 tablespoon olive oil
- 1 cup beef broth
- salt, pepper, to taste

Instructions:

1. Add oil to Instant Pot and press "Sauté" button. Add pork and cook for 2-3 minutes.
2. Add chime peppers to the Instant pot, season with salt and pepper. Cook for 2-3 additional minutes mixing from time to time.
3. Press "Keep warm/Cancel" button and add stock, onion, garlic, coconut milk, curry powder, Sriracha sauce, more salt and pepper.
4. Close the cover, and turn the vent to "Sealed".
5. Press "Manual" button, set the clock for 15 minutes and set "Strain" to high.
6. Once the clock is up, press "Drop" button and permit the strain to be delivered normally, until the float valve drops down.
7. *Open the lid.*
   NOTE: Make sure the tension is completely delivered prior to opening

the top, so you don't get burnt.

Nutritional info:
Calories: 510
Fats (g): 33.4
Fiber (g): 2.2 Net carbs (g): 8.2
Protein (g): 43.8

Apple Pork Tenderloin

Cooking time: 17 minutes
Servings: 6

Ingredients:

- 2 pounds pork loin
- 1 tablespoon olive oil

- ½ cup apple sauce, no sugar added
- ¼ cup coconut aminos
- 2 apples, sliced
- 1 red onion, sliced
- 2 garlic cloves, minced
- ½ cup beef broth
- 1 sprig rosemary
- 2 sprigs thyme
- ½ teaspoon Italian seasoning
- salt, pepper, to taste

Instructions:

1. Add oil to Instant Pot and press "Sauté" button. Season pork with salt and pepper and add to the Instant pot, cook on each side until brown. Move it to a plate.
2. Add more oil to the Instant pot if necessary and add onion. Cook for 2-3 moment until soft.
3. Add garlic and cook for 1 more moment. Add apples and sauté for 1 more minute.
4. Add pork flank on top of onion and apples, press "Keep warm/Cancel" button. Add fruit purée, coconut aminos, meat stock, rosemary, thyme, Italian flavoring, salt and pepper.
5. Close the cover, and turn the vent to "Sealed".
6. Press "Manual" button, set the clock for 12 minutes and set "Tension" to low.
7. Once the clock is up, press "Drop" button and permit the strain to be delivered normally, until the float valve drops down.
8. Open the lid.
   NOTE: Make sure the strain is completely delivered prior to opening the top, so you don't get burnt.
9. Slice the tenderloin into emblems and present with the fluid from the cooker.

Nutritional info:

Calories: 448
Fats (g): 23.8
Fiber (g): 2.5
Net carbs (g): 14.6
Protein (g): 42.2

Pork Chops with Bacon and Brussels

Cooking time: 20 minutes
Servings: 4

Ingredients:

- 4 pork bone-in chops 1
- tablespoon olive oil
- ¼ cup apple sauce, no sugar added 1
- cup chicken or beef broth
- 1 teaspoon Dijon mustard 2
- garlic cloves, minced
- ½ onion, chopped
- ½ tablespoon balsamic vinegar 7
- oz Brussels sprout, halved
- 2 bacon sliced, cooked, crumbled 1
- sprig rosemary
- 2 sprigs thyme
- salt, pepper, to taste

Instructions:

1. Add oil to Instant Pot and press "Sauté" button. Season pork hacks with salt and pepper and add to the Instant pot, cook on each side until brown. Move it to a plate.
2. Add more oil to the Instant pot if necessary and add onion and garlic. Cook for 2-3 minutes.
3. Add Brussels sprouts, rosemary, thyme and sauté for 2-3

additional minutes.

4. Add pork hacks on top of onion and Brussels sprouts, press "Keep warm/Cancel" button. Add fruit purée, stock, Dijon mustard, balsamic vinegar, salt and pepper.
5. Close the cover, and turn the vent to "Sealed".
6. Press "Manual" button, set the clock for 13 minutes and set "Tension" to high.
7. Once the clock is up, press "Drop" button and permit the strain to be delivered normally, until the float valve drops down.
8. Open the lid.
   NOTE: Make sure the strain is completely delivered prior to opening the top, so you don't get burnt.

Nutritional info:

Calories: 380

Fats (g): 21.9

Fiber (g): 2.6 Net

carbs (g): 7.8

Protein (g): 38.7

Pork Chops with Mushroom Cream Soup

Cooking time: 25 minutes

Servings: 4

Ingredients:

- 4 thick bone-in pork chops
- 2 tablespoons vegetable oil
- 1 ½ cups water
- ½ teaspoon lemon pepper
- salt, to taste
- 1 cup homemade stock
- 3 tablespoons organic grass-fed butter, melted
- ½ cup mushrooms, cut into small pieces, sautéed
-

- 1 tablespoon coconut milk
- 1/8 teaspoon garlic powder
- ¼ teaspoon sea salt
- a pinch of black pepper
- 2 tablespoons almond flour

Instructions:

1. First cook the Paleo consolidated cream of mushroom soup. Blend stock and almond flour in a bowl. Blend well with the goal that you don't get lumps.
2. Add margarine, milk, ocean salt, dark pepper and garlic powder, whisk well.
3. Stir in mushrooms. You have 1 container of consolidated cream of mushroom soup now.
4. Season the meat with lemon pepper.
5. Press "Sauté" button on the tension cooker, add oil and hotness it up.
6. Cook the meat for 2-3 minutes each side with the top open. Move seared meat to a plate.
7. Pour mushroom soup to the Instant pot. Mix for 1-2 minutes, press "Keep warm/Cancel" button and set the meat back to the cooker.
8. Close the cover. Press "Manual" button, set the clock for 20 minutes and set "Tension" to high.
9. Once the clock is up, press "Drop" button and permit the strain to be delivered normally, for around 10 minutes. Then, at that point, perform fast release.
10. Open the lid.

NOTE: Make sure the strain is completely delivered prior to opening the cover, so you don't get burnt.

Nutritional info:

Calories: 333

Fats (g): 28.1

Fiber (g): 0.3 Net carbs (g): 0.9
Protein (g): 18.6

Mediterranean Pork

Cooking time: 35 minutes

Servings: 6

Ingredients:

- 2 pounds pork tenderloin, sliced
- 1 tablespoon olive oil
- 1 tablespoon raw honey
- ¼ cup balsamic vinegar
- 3 garlic cloves, minced
- ½ teaspoon oregano
- ½ teaspoon dried rosemary
- 1 onion, sliced

- 3 oz olives, sliced
- 1 zucchini, sliced
- 1 cup water
- salt, pepper, to taste

Instructions:

1. Mix honey, vinegar, garlic, oregano, rosemary, salt and pepper in a bowl. Pour the marinade over pork cuts and marinade for 30 minutes in a fridge.
2. Add oil to Instant Pot and press "Sauté" button. Add pork cuts and cook on each side for 3-4 minutes.
3. Press "Keep warm/Cancel" button, add onion, olives, zucchini, water, salt and pepper to the Instant pot.
4. Close the top, and turn the vent to "Sealed".
5. Press "Manual" button, set the clock for 20 minutes and set "Strain" to high.
6. Once the clock is up, press "Drop" button and permit the strain to be delivered normally, until the float valve drops down.
7. Open the lid.
   NOTE: Make sure the tension is completely delivered prior to opening the cover, so you don't get burnt.
8. Serve with salad.

Nutritional info:

Calories: 281

Fats (g): 19.3

Fiber (g): 1.3

Net carbs (g): 7.3

Protein (g): 40.4

Pork Ribs BBQ

Cooking time: 55 minutes

Servings: 8

Ingredients:

- 3 ½ pounds pork ribs
- ½ cup chicken stock
- 2 tablespoons olive oil
- 2 teaspoons paprika
- 1 teaspoon onion powder
- 1 teaspoon garlic powder
- salt, black pepper, to taste

For Paleo BBQ sauce (1 cup):

- 1 cup organic tomato sauce
- ½ cup chicken bone broth or water
- ½ cup apple cider vinegar
- 1/3 cup raw honey
- 2 teaspoons paprika
- ½ teaspoon onion powder
- 1 teaspoon Dijon mustard
- salt and pepper, to taste

Instructions:

1. To make BBQ sauce, basically blend every one of the fixings in a pot, heat to the point of boiling and stew for 30 minutes.
2. Add oil to Instant Pot and press "Sauté" button. Season pork ribs with salt, pepper, paprika, onion powder, garlic powder and add to the Instant pot, cook until brown.
3. Press "Keep warm/Cancel" button, add chicken stock and ½ cup of BBQ sauce.

4. Close the top, and turn the vent to "Sealed".
5. Press "Manual" button, set the clock for 50 minutes and set "Tension" to high.
6. Once the clock is up, press "Drop" button and permit the strain to be delivered normally, until the float valve drops down.
7. Open the lid.
   NOTE: Make sure the strain is completely delivered prior to opening the top, so you don't get burnt.
8. Serve the ribs with more BBQ sauce.

Nutritional info:
Calories: 632
Fats (g): 38.9
Fiber (g): 1
Net carbs (g): 12.7
Protein (g): 53.4

Lime Lemongrass Pork

Cooking time: 35 minutes
Servings: 4

Ingredients:

- 2 pounds pork shoulder, cubed or shredded
- 1 tablespoon olive oil
- 3 teaspoons raw honey
- 1 cup chicken stock
- 1 lime, juiced

For marinade:

- 2 stalks lemongrass, inner part
- 1 shallot, chopped
- 5 garlic cloves
- ¼ cup fish sauce

- 2 tablespoons olive oil
- ground black pepper, to taste

Instructions:

1. Add all marinade fixings to a blender and heartbeat till smooth. Pour the marinade over the pork and marinade for 3-4 hours or overnight.
2. Add oil to the Instant pot and press "Sauté" button. Add honey and mix for 30 seconds, add pork and cook for 2-3 minutes.
3. Press "Drop" button, add stock and close the top, turn the vent to "Sealed".
4. Press "Manual" button, set the clock for 28 minutes and set "Tension" to high.
5. Once the clock is up, press "Drop" button and permit the strain to be delivered normally, until the float valve drops down.
6. Open the lid.
   NOTE: Make sure the strain is completely delivered prior to opening the top, so you don't get burnt.
7. Serve with lime juice.

Nutritional info:

Calories: 528

Fats (g): 39.5

Fiber (g): 0.4 Net

carbs (g): 6.1

Protein (g): 36.2

Pork Chops with Veggies

Cooking time: 20 minutes
Servings: 4

Ingredients:

- 1 cup baby carrots, chopped
- 2 cups cauliflower florets
- 1 onion, chopped
- 4 ¾ inch thick bone-in pork chops
- 3 tablespoons Worcestershire
- sauce salt and pepper, to taste
- 1 cup vegetable broth
- ¼ cup grass-fed butter

Instructions:

1. Generously season the meat with salt and pepper.
2. Press "Sauté" button on the strain cooker, liquefy 2 teaspoons butter.
3. Add the meat and cook with the cover open on all sides until brown. Move the meat to a plate.

4. Melt the remainder of the spread in the cooker. Sauté onion and carrots for several minutes.
5. Stir in the Worcestershire sauce and add the stock. Return the cooked meat to the pot. Press "Keep warm/Cancel" button.
6. Place the liner container to the tension cooker and put the cauliflower florets in it. Close the top, and turn the vent to "Sealed".
7. Press "Manual" button, set the clock for 13 minutes and set "Strain" to high.
8. Once the clock is up, press "Drop" button and permit the strain to be delivered normally, until the float valve drops down.
9. Open the lid.

NOTE: Make sure the tension is completely delivered prior to opening the top, so you don't get burnt.

Nutritional info:

Calories: 283

Fats (g): 28.4

Fiber (g): 2.2 Net

carbs (g): 9.8

Protein (g): 13.7

Halibut Fish Stew

Cooking time: 15 minutes

Servings: 4

Ingredients:

- 1 pound halibut, boneless and cubed
- 1 lime juice
- 1 jalapeno pepper, seedless, chopped
- 1 yellow onion, chopped
- 1 yellow pepper, chopped
- 2 garlic cloves, minced

- 1 teaspoon paprika
- salt, pepper, to taste
- 2 cups chicken stock
- 2 cups tomatoes, chopped
- 1 can (15 oz) coconut milk

Instructions:

1. Pour lime juice to a bowl, add fish. Marinate while you cook other ingredients.
2. Press "Sauté" button on the tension cooker, add oil and hotness it up.
3. Add onions and peppers, cook with the cover open for 3-5 minutes until onion is delicate. Add garlic and sauté for 30 seconds.
4. Add tomatoes, stock, salt, pepper and paprika to the pot. Cook for 2-3 additional minutes blending well.
5. Press "Keep warm/Cancel" button. Add fish with lime juice marinade and coconut milk.
6. Close the top, and turn the vent to "Fixed". Press "Manual" button, set the clock for 10 minutes and set "Strain" to high.
7. Once the clock is up press "Drop" button and turn the steam discharge handle to "Venting" position for fast delivery, until the float valve drops down.
8. Open the lid.

NOTE: Make sure the tension is completely delivered prior to opening the top, so you don't get burnt.

Nutritional info:

Calories: 380

Fats (g): 29

Fiber (g): 3.8

Net carbs (g): 14.6

Protein (g): 19.5

Asian Style Salmon

Cooking time: 5 minutes
Servings: 2

Ingredients:

- 2 salmon fillets, boneless
- 1 cup water
- a pinch of sea salt and black pepper
- 2 tablespoons coconut aminos
- 8 ounces broccoli
- 8 ounces cauliflower florets
- 2 tablespoons lemon juice 1
- teaspoon sesame seeds

Instructions:

1. Mix coconut aminos and lemon juice in a bowl, whisk well.
2. Season salmon filets with salt and pepper. Put the fish, broccoli and cauliflower florets onto a plate and pour the lemon blend on top. Let marinate for 10-15 minutes.
3. Pour water into your moment pot, add the liner bushel. Add salmon and veggies to the container and close the lid.
4. Close the top, and turn the vent to "Fixed". Press "Manual" button, set the clock for 5 minutes and set "Strain" to high.
5. Once the clock is up press "Drop" button and turn the steam discharge handle to "Venting" position for fast delivery, until the float valve drops down.
6. Open the lid.
   NOTE: Make sure the tension is completely delivered prior to opening the cover, so you don't get burnt.

Nutritional info:

Calories: 315

Fats (g): 22.3

Fiber (g): 5
Net carbs (g): 14.2
Protein (g): 30.4

Tomato Shrimps

Cooking time: 5 minutes

Servings: 4

Ingredients:

- 1 pound shrimps, cooked, peeled and deveined
- 2 tablespoons olive oil
- 1 garlic clove, minced
- ¼ teaspoon oregano, dried
- 1 tablespoon parsley, chopped
- 1/3 cup water
- 10 ounces canned tomatoes, chopped
- 1/3 cup tomato paste

Instructions:

1. Press "Sauté" button on the strain cooker, add oil and hotness it up.
2. Add garlic, mix and brown for 2 minutes.
3. Add shrimp, tomato glue, tomatoes, water, oregano and parsley, mix for 1 more minute.
4. Press "Keep warm/Cancel" button. Close the top, and turn the vent to "Sealed".
5. Press "Manual" button, set the clock for 3 minutes and set "Tension" to high.
6. Once the clock is up press "Drop" button and turn the steam discharge handle to "Venting" position for fast delivery, until the float valve drops down.
7. Open the lid.
   NOTE: Make sure the strain is completely delivered prior to opening the top, so you don't get burnt.
8. Serve shrimps with salad on the side.

Nutritional info:

Calories: 227

Fats (g): 19.2

Fiber (g): 1.8

Net carbs (g): 9

Protein (g): 27.5

Steamed Crab Legs

Cooking time: 3 minutes

Servings: 4

Ingredients:

- 2 pounds crab legs
- 4 lemon wedges
- 1/3 cup ghee, melted
- 1 cup water

Instructions:

1. Pour water into your Instant pot and spot a trivet in the bottom.
2. Add crab legs, close the cover, and turn the vent to "Sealed".
3. Press "Manual" button, set the clock for 3 minutes and set "Strain" to high.
4. Once the clock is up press "Drop" button and turn the steam discharge handle to "Venting" position for speedy delivery, until the float valve drops down.
5. Open the lid.
   NOTE: Make sure the tension is completely delivered prior to opening the top, so you don't get burnt.
6. Serve with softened ghee and lemon wedges.

Nutritional info:

Calories: 402

Fats (g): 20.8

Fiber (g): 0.2 Net

carbs (g): 0.7

Protein (g): 27.6

Paleo Cod Fillet

Cooking time: 5 minutes

Servings: 4

Ingredients:

- 1 pound cod fillets, cut into medium strips
- 2 eggs
- 2 cups almond flour
- a pinch of sea salt and black pepper
- ¼ teaspoon paprika
- 1 cup water

Instructions:

1. Mix flour, salt, pepper and paprika in a bowl.
2. Whisk eggs in a different bowl.
3. Dip fish strips in eggs and afterward flour mix.
4. Add water to your Instant pot, put a liner bushel there
5. Add fish strip, close the top, and turn the vent to "Sealed".
6. Press "Manual" button, set the clock for 5 minutes and set "Tension" to high.
7. Once the clock is up press "Drop" button and turn the steam discharge handle to "Venting" position for fast delivery, until the float valve drops down.
8. Open the lid.
NOTE: Make sure the tension is completely delivered prior to opening the top, so you don't get burnt.

Nutritional info:
Calories: 144

Fats (g): 13.5

Fiber (g): 0.1 Net carbs (g): 0.2

Protein (g): 27.8

Shrimps with Coconut Lemon Sauce

Cooking time: 7 minutes

Servings: 8

Ingredients:

- 2 pound shrimp, deveined, tails off
- 2/3 cup (5 oz) water or vegetable or chicken broth
- 2/3 cup almond milk
- 1 tablespoon olive oil
- 1 lemon, juice
- 1 tablespoon garlic, minced
- salt, pepper, to taste
- 1 medium lemon, sliced for serving
- 1 tablespoon arrowroot starch

Instructions:

1. Press "Sauté" button on the tension cooker, add oil and hotness it up.
2. Add garlic and sauté for 1 moment. Add shrimps and pour lemon juice over them. Sauté for 3-4 minutes.
3. Press "Keep warm/Cancel" button. Add stock and almond milk, salt and pepper to taste.
4. Press "Manual" button, set the clock for 3 minutes and set "Tension" to high.
5. Once the clock is up press "Drop" button and turn the steam discharge handle to "Venting" position for speedy delivery, until the float valve drops down. Open the lid.
6. Press "Sauté" button once more. Add arrowroot starch and mix well until the sauce thickens.

Nutritional info:

Calories: 167

Fats (g): 14.8

Fiber (g): 0.5 Net

carbs (g): 3.3

Protein (g): 26.5

Thai Scallops with Oranges

Cooking time: 6 minutes

Servings: 4

Ingredients:

- 1 pound sea scallops, cleaned
- 1 jalapeno pepper, seedless and minced
- ¼ cup extra virgin olive oil
- ¼ cup rice vinegar
- ¼ teaspoon mustard
- salt, black pepper, to the taste
- a pinch cayenne pepper

- 1 tablespoon vegetable oil
- 1/3 cup water or broth
- 2 oranges, sliced

Instructions:

1. Pulse jalapeno with olive oil, mustard, dark pepper, salt and vinegar in a blender.
2. Season scallops with cayenne pepper.
3. Press "Sauté" button on the strain cooker, add oil and hotness it up.
4. Add scallops and cook them with the cover open for 3 minutes on each side.
5. Press "Keep warm/Cancel" button. Add water or stock, jalapeno sauce, orange cuts and close the top, turn the vent to "Sealed".
6. Press "Manual" button, set the clock for 3 minutes and set "Strain" to high.
7. Once the clock is up press "Drop" button and turn the steam discharge handle to "Venting" position for speedy delivery, until the float valve

   drops down. Open the cover and enjoy.

Nutritional info:

Calories: 293

Fats (g): 27.1

Fiber (g): 2.4

Net carbs (g): 13.8

Protein (g): 20

Scallops with Mushrooms and Spinach

Cooking time: 5 minutes

Servings: 2

Ingredients:

- 1 pound medium sized scallops, cleaned
-

- 7 oz mushrooms, sliced
- 8 oz spinach, washed, chopped
- 3 tablespoons ghee, melted
- 2 tablespoons coconut oil
- 2-3 fresh nutmegs, grated
- 1/3 cup water
- sea salt, pepper, to taste

Instructions:

1. Press "Sauté" button on the strain cooker, add coconut oil and hotness it up.
2. Season scallops with salt and pepper. Add scallops and cook with the cover open the two sides until marginally carmelized. Move the scallops to a plate.
3. Add ghee to the cooker and hotness it up. Add mushrooms and sauté for 1-2 minutes.
4. Add spinach and sauté for 1 more minute.
5. Press "Keep warm/Cancel" button. Add scallops to the pot, season with salt and pepper to taste and add ground nutmeg. Add water.
6. Press "Manual" button, set the clock for 3 minutes and set "Tension" to high.
7. Once the clock is up press "Drop" button and turn the steam discharge handle to "Venting" position for speedy delivery, until the float valve drops down. Open the cover and enjoy.

Nutritional info:

Calories: 250

Fats (g): 28

Fiber (g): 2.1 Net

carbs (g): 6.6

Protein (g): 17.6

Paleo Shrimp Paella

Cooking time: 7 minutes
Servings: 4

Ingredients:

- 1 cup cauliflower rice
- 20 big shrimp, peeled and deveined
- a pinch of red pepper, crushed
- ¼ cup parsley, chopped
- sea salt and black pepper, to taste
- ¼ cup ghee
- a pinch of saffron
- 1 ½ cups water
- 1 lemon, juice
- 4 garlic cloves, minced

Instructions:

1. Press "Sauté" button on the tension cooker. Add water.
2. Add rice to the Instant pot.
3. Add shrimps, ghee, parsley, salt, pepper, red pepper, lemon juice, saffron and garlic, mix for 1-2 minutes with the cover open. Press "Keep warm/Cancel" button.
4. Close the cover, and turn the vent to "Sealed".
5. Press "Manual" button, set the clock for 5 minutes and set "Tension" to high.
6. Once the clock is up press "Drop" button and turn the steam discharge handle to "Venting" position for speedy delivery, until the float valve drops down.
7. Open the lid.

NOTE: Make sure the strain is completely delivered prior to opening the top, so you don't get burnt.

8. Serve finished off with parsley.

Nutritional info:
Calories: 192
Fats (g): 14.3
Fiber (g): 1
Net carbs (g): 7.6
Protein (g): 9

Stuffed Squid

Cooking time: 20 minutes
Servings: 4

Ingredients:

- 7 ounces vegetable stock
- 3 tablespoons coconut aminos
- 10-12 medium-sized squids, tentacles and heads removed, tentacles chopped
- 1 cup cauliflower rice
-

- salt, pepper, to taste
- ¼ teaspoon chili powder
- 2 teaspoons olive oil

Instructions:

1. Press "Sauté" button on the tension cooker. Add oil and hotness it up.
2. Mix cleaved arms with cauliflower rice and add to the Instant pot. Mix for 3-4 minutes with the cover open, add salt and pepper to taste. Press "Keep warm/Cancel" button.
3. Stuff squid with this mixture.
4. Put stuffed squids into your Instant pot, add aminos and stock, mix well, add salt and pepper if necessary and bean stew powder.
5. Close the top and turn the vent to "Sealed".
6. Press "Manual" button, set the clock for 15 minutes and set "Tension" to high.
7. Once the clock is up press "Drop" button and turn the steam discharge handle to "Venting" position for fast delivery, until the float valve drops down. Open the lid.

Nutritional info:
Calories: 189
Fats (g): 15.9
Fiber (g): 0.3 Net
carbs (g): 7.7
Protein (g): 13.4

Butternut Squash and Chard Soup

Cooking time: 20 minutes
Servings: 4

Ingredients:

- 1 tablespoon olive oil
- 1 yellow onion, chopped
-

- 3 big carrots, chopped
- 3 celery stalks, chopped
- 4 thyme sprigs
- a pinch of salt and black pepper
- 1 teaspoon rosemary, chopped
- 4 cups Swiss chard leaves, chopped
- 2 cups butternut squash, peeled and cubed
- 4 garlic cloves, minced
- 1 cup coconut milk
- 1 cup water

Instructions:

1. Press "Sauté" button on the strain cooker. Add oil and hotness it up.
2. Add onions and sauté for 1 moment. Add carrots and celery, mix and cook for 2 additional minutes.
3. Add thyme spring, salt, pepper, butternut squash, garlic and rosemary, mix well. Close the cover, and turn the vent to "Sealed".
4. Add coconut milk and water. Close the cover and turn the vent to "Sealed".
5. Press "Soup" button, set "Strain" to high and clock for 20 minutes.
6. Once the clock is up press "Drop" button and turn the steam discharge handle to "Venting" position for fast delivery, until the float valve

   drops down. Open the lid.
7. Remove thyme springs, add Swiss chard and press "Sauté" button. Mix for 1-2 minutes and serve.

Nutritional info:

Calories: 249

Fats (g): 18.1

Fiber (g): 3.8

Net carbs (g): 18.6

Protein (g): 3.8

Mushroom Stew

Cooking time: 25 minutes
Servings: 4

Ingredients:

- 8 ounces shiitake mushrooms, roughly chopped
- 4 ounces white mushrooms, roughly chopped
- 1 tablespoon ginger, grated
- ½ cup red onion, finely chopped
- ½ cup celery, chopped
- ½ cup carrot, chopped
- 5 garlic cloves, minced
- salt and black pepper, to taste
- ¼ teaspoon dried oregano
-

- 4 tomatoes, chopped
- ¼ cup water
- 1 ½ teaspoon turmeric powder
- ¼ cup basil leaves, chopped

Instructions:

1. Press "Sauté" button on the tension cooker. Add onion, celery, carrot, ginger and garlic, mix and sauté for 5 minutes.
2. Add tomatoes, salt, pepper, turmeric, oregano and water, mix well. Press "Keep warm/Cancel" button.
3. Close the cover and turn the vent to "Sealed".
4. Press "Manual" button, set the clock for 18 minutes and set "Strain" to high.
5. Once the clock is up press "Drop" button and turn the steam discharge handle to "Venting" position for speedy delivery, until the float valve drops down. Open the lid.
6. Add basil, mix for 1 moment and serve.

Nutritional info:

Calories: 86

Fats (g): 11.7

Fiber (g): 3.3 Net

carbs (g): 9.5

Protein (g): 13.7

Cauliflower Soup

Cooking time: 30 minutes

Servings: 5

Ingredients:

- 1 cauliflower head, florets separated, chopped
- 1 cup carrots, diced
- 1 onion, diced

- 1 tablespoon ginger, grated
- 3 garlic cloves, minced
- 4 cups vegetable broth
- 1 can coconut milk
- 3 tomatoes, chopped
- 2 tablespoons curry powder
- salt, pepper, to taste

Instructions:

1. Press "Sauté" button on the strain cooker. Add oil and hotness it up. Add carrots and onion, cook blending for 2-3 minutes with the top open.
2. Add cauliflower, garlic, ginger and curry powder, mix well. Press "Keep warm/Cancel" button.
3. Add stock and coconut milk, close the top and turn the vent to "Sealed".
4. Press "Soup" button, set "Strain" to high and the clock for 20 minutes.
5. Once the clock is up press "Drop" button and turn the steam discharge handle to "Venting" position for fast delivery, until the float valve drops down. Open the lid.

Nutritional info

Calories: 200

Fats (g): 23.2

Fiber (g): 5.3

Net carbs (g): 16.1

Protein (g): 17.6

Plain Tender Kale

Cooking time: 5 minutes

Servings: 3

Ingredients:

- 10 ounces kale, cleaned, stems removed, chopped
- 2 tablespoons olive oil
- salt, to taste
- 1 onion, thinly sliced
- 5 garlic cloves, peeled and chopped
- ¼ teaspoon red pepper flakes
- 1/3 cup water
- 3 tablespoons lemon juice

Instructions:

1. Press "Sauté" button on the strain cooker. Add oil and hotness it up.
2. Add onions and sauté for 1-2 minutes. Add garlic and cook for 30 seconds.
3. Add kale, salt and pepper, mix well. Press "Keep warm/Cancel" button. Add water, close the cover and turn the vent to "Sealed".
4. Press "Manual" button, set the clock for 3 minutes and set "Strain" to high.
5. Once the clock is up press "Drop" button and turn the steam discharge handle to "Venting" position for fast delivery, until the float valve drops down.
6. Open the top. Sprinkle with lemon juice and serve.

Nutritional info

Calories: 153
Fats (g): 9.6
Fiber (g): 2.4
Net carbs (g): 13.3
Protein (g): 23.7

Steamed Artichokes

Cooking time: 20 minutes

Servings: 5

Ingredients:

- 1 lemon wedge
- 2 (5 1/2 oz. each) medium-sized whole artichokes, rinsed, stem & top third removed
- 1 cup water

Instructions

1. Use a lemon wedge to rub each slice top of the artichokes to stop browning.
2. Place a liner bushel or a steam rack into Instant Pot.
3. Put the artichokes into the liner bin and add water.
4. Close the cover and turn the vent to "Sealed".
5. Press "Manual" button, set the clock for 20 minutes and set "Tension" to high.

6. Once the clock is up, press "Drop" button and permit strain to be delivered normally, until the float valve drops down.
7. Open the lid.

NOTE: Make sure the tension is completely delivered prior to opening the top, so you don't get burnt.

8. Carefully take the artichokes out with utensils and present with wanted plunging sauce.

Nutritional info:
Calories: 64
Fats (g): 12.4
Fiber (g): 7
Net carbs (g): 13
Protein (g): 13.5

Olives and Eggplant Spread
Cooking time: 20 minutes
Servings: 5

Ingredients:

- 2 pounds eggplant, peeled from one side only, chopped
- 1 cup water
- 4 tablespoons olive oil
- ¼ cup black olives, pitted
- 1 tablespoon tahini
- 4 garlic cloves
- ¼ cup freshly squeezed lemon juice
- 1 teaspoon salt
- 1 tablespoon fresh thyme leaves

Instructions:

1. Press "Sauté" button on the strain cooker. Add oil and hotness it up.

2. Add eggplant, fry and caramelize from all sides, for around 5 minutes with the cover open. Press "Keep warm/Cancel" button.
3. Add garlic, water and salt. Close the cover and turn the vent to "Sealed".
4. Press "Manual" button, set the clock for 3 minutes and set "Tension" to high.
5. Once the clock is up, press "Drop" button and permit the strain to be delivered normally, until the float valve drops down. Open the lid.
6. Discard the greater part of the fluid from the pot. Get garlic cloves and eliminate the skin. Set them back to the pot, add lemon juice, dark olives and tahini.
7. Use an inundation blender to make a puree. Move to a bowl. Sprinkle with a hint of olive oil, dark olives and thyme before serving.

Nutritional info:

Calories: 175

Fats (g): 14

Fiber (g): 7.2

Net carbs (g): 13.1

Protein (g): 12.7

Stir-Fried Broccoli

Cooking time: 10 minutes

Servings: 4

Ingredients:

- 1 broccoli head, stems trimmed and cut into
- florets 1 garlic clove, crushed and peeled
- ½ cup vegetable stock
- 2 tablespoons soy sauce
- 2 tablespoons sesame
-

oil salt, to taste

- 1 small slice fresh ginger

Instructions:

1. Press "Sauté" button on the strain cooker. Add oil and hotness it up.
2. Add garlic and ginger, cook for 2 minutes.
3. Add broccoli, salt and pepper, cook for 3 additional minutes. Press "Keep warm/Cancel" button and eliminate vegetables from the Instant pot.
4. Place the liner bin into the Instant pot. Pour stock and soy sauce to the pot.
5. Put broccoli into the liner basket.
6. Close the top and turn the vent to "Fixed". Press "Manual" button, set the clock for 5 minutes and set "Strain" to high.
7. Once the clock is up, press "Drop" button and permit strain to be delivered normally, until the float valve drops down.
8. Open the lid.

NOTE: Make sure the tension is completely delivered prior to opening the top, so you don't get burnt.

Nutritional info:

Calories: 83

Fats (g): 7

Fiber (g): 1.4 Net

carbs (g): 4.2

Protein (g): 11.9

Quick Zucchini Curry Soup

Cooking time: 10 minutes
Servings: 4

Ingredients:

- 2 pounds zucchini,
- chopped 1 tablespoon raw honey
- 1 tablespoon curry paste
- 1 can coconut milk
- 15 oz vegetable stock

Instructions:

1. Put every one of the fixings to the Instant pot: zucchini, honey, curry glue, coconut milk and vegetable stock.
2. Close the cover and turn the vent to "Sealed".
3. Press "Manual" button, set the clock for 10 minutes and set

"Tension" to high.
4. Once the clock is up, press "Drop" button and permit strain to be delivered normally, until the float valve drops down. Open the lid.
5. Puree the soup with blender or in some other food processor. Add salt and pepper to taste if needed.

Nutritional info:

Calories: 222

Fats (g): 17

Fiber (g): 2.4

Net carbs (g): 10.3

Protein (g): 14.8

Vegetable Stew Ratatouille

Cooking time: 10 minutes

Servings: 4

Ingredients:

- 2 tablespoons parsley, minced
- 1 eggplant, cut into cubes, skin removed
- 2 tomatoes, chopped
- ¼ cup vegetable stock
- 2 cloves garlic, minced
- 2 green peppers, cut into strips, seeded
- 1 onion, sliced
- 2 zucchinis, sliced
- 4 tablespoons coconut oil
- salt, pepper, to taste

Instructions:

1. Press "Sauté" button on the tension cooker. Add 2 tablespoons oil and hotness it up.

2. Add garlic and onion, cook for 2-3 minutes.
3. Add remaining oil and add eggplant, peppers and zucchini. Cook until vegetables are delicate. Press "Keep warm/Cancel" button.
4. Add parsley, vegetable stock and tomatoes, salt and pepper to taste.
5. Close the top and turn the vent to "Sealed".
6. Press "Manual" button, set the clock for 4 minutes and set "Tension" to high.
7. Once the clock is up, press "Drop" button and permit strain to be delivered normally, until the float valve drops down. Open the lid.
8. Simmer the dish for 2 minutes. Serve warm.

Nutritional info:

Calories: 200

Fats (g): 14.3

Fiber (g): 4.7

Net carbs (g): 16.6

Protein (g): 3.9

Curried Carrot Soup

Cooking time: 10 minutes

Servings: 5

Ingredients:

- 1 pound carrots, rinsed and diced
- 2 tablespoons extra virgin olive
- oil 2 garlic cloves, minced
- 1 onion, chopped
- 2 teaspoons fresh turmeric, grated
- ½ teaspoon ground cumin
- 2 teaspoons curry powder
- ½ teaspoon sea salt
- ¼ cup toasted pumpkin seeds
- ½ cauliflower head, florets chopped
-

- 1 tablespoon lemon juice
- ½ cup apple juice
- 5 ½ cups vegetable broth
- parsley leaves, cilantro or ground chilies (for garnishing)

Instructions:

1. Press "Sauté" button on the strain cooker. Add oil and hotness it up.
2. Add garlic, onion and carrots, cook for 3-5 minutes.
3. Add curry powder, salt, cumin and turmeric. Cook for one more moment while blending regularly. Press "Keep warm/Cancel" button.
4. Add squeezed apple, stock and cauliflower. Close the top and turn the vent to "Sealed".
5. Press "Manual" button, set the clock for 7 minutes and set "Pressure" to high.
6. Once the clock is up, press "Drop" button and permit strain to be delivered normally, until the float valve drops down. Open the lid.
7. Puree soup utilizing a blender. Process until smooth. Season with salt and add the lemon juice.
8. Garnish with toasted pumpkin seeds and parsley leaves (or ground chilies) before serving.

Nutritional info:

Calories: 201
Fats (g): 15.6
Fiber (g): 4.2 Net
carbs (g): 16
Protein (g): 18.9

Cauliflower Mushroom Risotto

Cooking Time: 10 minutes

Servings: 4

Ingredients

- 1 tablespoon olive oil
- 2 garlic cloves, minced
- 4 baby bella mushrooms
- 1 cup vegetable broth
- 1 large cauliflower head, broke into florets, blended till riced
- ¼ cup coconut milk
- 1 teaspoon chervil, dried
- salt, pepper, to taste

Instructions

1. Press "Sauté" button on your Instant Pot, set "Temperature"

to medium. Add oil and hotness it up for 1-2 minutes.
2. Add garlic and mushrooms. Sauté for 3-4 minutes. Press "Keep warm/Cancel" button.
3. Add cauliflower, stock, salt, and pepper.
4. Close the cover, and turn the vent to "Sealed".
5. Press "Steam" button, set the clock for 5 minutes and set "Strain" to high.
6. Once the clock is up press "Drop" button and turn the steam discharge handle to "Venting" position for fast delivery, until the float valve drops down.
7. Open the top and let the dish cool down a little. Add coconut milk, mix well. Add salt if needed.

Nutritional info:

Calories: 101

Fats (g): 12.6

Fiber (g): 2.5 Net

carbs (g): 6.6

Protein (g): 3.7

Plain Banana Bread

Cooking time: 30 minutes

Servings: 6

Ingredients:

- 1 egg
- 2 bananas, mashed
- 1/3 cup ghee
- 2 cups almond flour
- 1/3 cup coconut milk
- 3 teaspoons lemon juice or white vinegar
- ¾ cup coconut sugar
- 1 teaspoon baking soda

- ½ teaspoon baking powder
- 2 cups water
- a pinch of salt

Instructions:

1. Mix coconut milk and lemon squeeze or white vinegar in a bowl.
2. Mix ghee and sugar, add egg and crushed bananas, blend well.
3. Mix flour, baking pop, baking powder and salt in a different bowl. Add to the ghee blend, blending constantly.
4. Slowly add coconut milk mixture.
5. Pour the batter into the lubed cake dish, ensure it will accommodate your Instant pot. For the container with aluminum foil, try to make a tight seal.
6. Place a trivet into the Instant pot, set the cake skillet on the trivet.
7. Close the top, and turn the vent to "Sealed".
8. Press "Manual" button, set the clock for 30 minutes and set "Strain" to high.
9. Once the clock is up, press "Drop" button and permit the strain to be delivered normally, until the float valve drops down. Open the lid.

NOTE: Make sure the strain is completely delivered prior to opening the cover, so you don't get burnt.

10. Remove the skillet and pour off overabundance dampness if any. Let cool and serve.

Nutritional info:

Calories: 267

Fats (g): 20.4

Fiber (g): 2.3 Net

carbs (g): 6.6

Protein (g): 13.7

Sweet Apple Crust

Cooking time: 8 minutes

Servings: 6

Ingredients:

- 6 apples, peeled, cut into bite size chunks
- ½ cup water
- 1 ¼ teaspoon nutmeg
- 1 ½ teaspoon cinnamon
- ½ cup raw honey
- 2 tablespoons grass fed butter, melted
- 2 cups almond flour
- ½ teaspoon salt
- cooking spray

Instructions:

1. Spray the moment pot skillet with a cooking shower. Set apples on the lower part of the tension cooker.
2. Sprinkle apples with nutmeg and cinnamon. Add water and honey.
3. Mix spread, flour and salt in a bowl.
4. Add the flour combination to the Instant pot. Close the cover, and turn the vent to "Sealed".
5. Press "Manual" button, set the clock for 8 minutes and set "Strain" to high.
6. Once the clock is up, press "Drop" button and permit the strain to be delivered normally, until the float valve drops down. Open the lid.
7. Serve apples hot.

Nutritional info:
Calories: 299
Fats (g): 18
Fiber (g): 6.9
Net carbs (g): 16.5
Protein (g): 18

Apple Cake

Cooking time: 28 minutes
Servings: 4

Ingredients:

- 4 apples, peeled, sliced
- 2 tablespoons lemon juice
- ½ cup almond flour
- 1/3 cup cassava flour
- ½ teaspoon baking powder
- 1/3 cup coconut oil
- a pinch of salt
- 1 teaspoon vanilla powder
- 1 tablespoon gelatin powder
- 3 tablespoons raw honey
- 2 cups water

Instructions:

1. Prepare a medium cake skillet, ensure it fits the Instant pot. Line it with the material paper.
2. Put apples on the lower part of the cake skillet, spread them uniformly. Sprinkle with lemon juice.
3. Mix almond flour, cassava flour, baking powder and salt in a bowl.
4. Mix coconut oil, honey and vanilla in a different bowl. Add gelatin powder and whisk well.
5. Mix flour combination with coconut oil blend and shape dough.
6. Pour batter over apples, spread it uniformly. For the skillet with aluminum foil, try to make a tight seal.
7. Add water to the Instant pot.
8. Place a trivet into the tension cooker, set the cake container on the trivet.
9. Close the cover, and turn the vent to "Sealed".
10. Press "Manual" button, set the clock for 28 minutes and set "Strain" to high.
11. Once the clock is up, press "Drop" button and permit the strain to be delivered normally, until the float valve drops down. Open the lid.
12. Turn the cake topsy turvy before serving.

Nutritional info:

Calories: 421

Fats (g): 20.7

Fiber (g): 6.9

Net carbs (g): 17.4

Protein (g): 16.8

Pumpkin Cake

Cooking time: 35 minutes

Servings: 5

Ingredients:

- 2 cups pumpkin puree
- 3 eggs
- ½ cup coconut milk
- ½ cup raw honey
- a pinch of salt
- 2 tablespoon pumpkin pie spice
- 1 cup water

Instructions:

1. Mix puree and eggs in a bowl or in a blender.
2. Add coconut milk, honey, zest and salt.
3. Grease a 6-inch round cake dish with a coconut-oil based splash.
4. Pour in the cake hitter, and cover firmly with foil.
5. Pour water into your tension cooker and supplement a trivet.
6. Place the cake container on the trivet, close the top, and turn the vent to "Sealed".
7. Press "Manual" button, set the clock for 35 minutes and set "Strain" to high.
8. Once the clock is up, press "Drop" button and permit the strain to be delivered normally, until the float valve drops down.
9. Open the lid.
   NOTE: Make sure the strain is completely delivered prior to opening the top, so you don't get burnt.
10. Let it cool and refrigerate for a few hours.

Nutritional info:

Calories: 237

Fats (g): 18.9

Fiber (g): 3.8

Net carbs (g): 28.9

Protein (g): 15.2

Coconut Cake

Cooking time: 35 minutes

Servings: 6

Ingredients:

- 1 cup coconut milk
- 2 whole eggs
- 3 egg whites
- 1/3 cup raw honey
- ¾ cup coconut flour
- 1 tablespoon vanilla extract
- 2 teaspoons baking powder
- ½ teaspoon baking soda
- a pinch of salt
- 1 cup water

Instructions:

1. Mix coconut milk, eggs, egg whites, honey and vanilla concentrate in a bowl.
2. Add flour, baking powder, baking pop and salt. Blend well until combined.
3. Grease a 6-inch round cake dish with a coconut-oil based spray.
4. Pour in the cake hitter, and cover firmly with foil.
5. Pour water into your tension cooker and addition a trivet.
6. Place the cake container on the trivet, close the top, and turn the vent to "Sealed".
7. Press "Manual" button, set the clock for 20 minutes and set "Strain" to high.
8. Once the clock is up, press "Drop" button and permit the strain to be delivered normally, until the float valve drops down.
9. Open the lid.
   NOTE: Make sure the tension is completely delivered prior to opening

the top, so you don't get burnt.

10. Take out the skillet and hang tight for 15-20 minutes. Turn the cake over on a serving dish.

Nutritional info:

Calories: 237

Fats (g): 12.3

Fiber (g): 6

Net carbs (g): 17.4

Protein (g): 26.3

Breakfast Mug Cake

Cooking time: 10 minutes

Servings: 4

Ingredients:

- 1 1/3 cup almond
-

flour 4 eggs
- 2 teaspoons vanilla
- extract 4 tablespoons
- maple syrup 2 cups water
- a pinch of salt

Instructions:
1. Mix every one of the fixings in a bowl.
2. Put the blend into 4 artisan containers (8 oz). Partition uniformly however ensure you don't overload the jars.
3. Add water to the Instant pot. Place a trivet into the tension cooker.
4. Put the mugs on the trivet. Close the cover, and turn the vent to "Sealed".
5. Press "Manual" button, set the clock for 10 minutes and set "Strain" to high.
6. Once the clock is up, press "Drop" button and permit the strain to be delivered normally, until the float valve drops down. Open the lid.
7. Once the clock is up press "Drop" button and turn the steam discharge handle to "Venting" position for fast delivery, until the float valve drops down.
8. Open the cover. Serve warm or chilled.

Nutritional info:

Calories: 181

Fats (g): 19.4

Fiber (g): 1

Net carbs (g): 15.7

Protein (g): 5.5

Printed in Great Britain
by Amazon